PREFACE

1. Scope

This publication establishes doctrine for planning, conducting, and assessing operational contract support integration and contractor management functions in support of joint operations. It provides standardized guidance and information related to integrating operational contract support and contractor management, defines and describes these two different, but directly related functions, and provides a basic discussion on contracting command and control organizational options. **This joint publication does not pertain to contracting support of routine, recurring (i.e., non-contingency) Department of Defense operations.** It also does not provide a significant discussion of construction-related contracting since this topic is covered in depth by Joint Publication 3-34, *Engineering Operations*.

2. Purpose

This publication has been prepared under the direction of the Chairman of the Joint Chiefs of Staff (CJCS). It sets forth joint doctrine to govern the activities and performance of the Armed Forces of the United States in joint operations and provides the doctrinal basis for interagency coordination and for US military involvement in multinational operations. It provides military guidance for the exercise of authority by combatant commanders and other joint force commanders (JFCs) and prescribes joint doctrine for operations, education, and training. It provides military guidance for use by the Armed Forces in preparing their appropriate plans. It is not the intent of this publication to restrict the authority of the JFC from organizing the force and executing the mission in a manner the JFC deems most appropriate to ensure unity of effort in the accomplishment of the overall objectives.

3. Application

a. Joint doctrine established in this publication applies to the commanders of combatant commands, subunified commands, joint task forces, subordinate components of these commands, the Services, and defense agencies in support of joint operations.

b. The guidance in this publication is authoritative; as such, this doctrine will be followed except when, in the judgment of the commander, exceptional circumstances dictate otherwise. If conflicts arise between the contents of this publication and the contents of Service publications, this publication will take precedence unless the CJCS, normally in coordination with the other members of the Joint Chiefs of Staff, has provided more current and specific guidance. Commanders of forces operating as part of a multinational (alliance or coalition) military command should follow multinational doctrine and procedures ratified by the United States. For doctrine and procedures not ratified by the United States, commanders should evaluate and follow the multinational command's doctrine and procedures, where applicable and consistent with US law, regulations, and doctrine.

For the Chairman of the Joint Chiefs of Staff:

STANLEY A. MCCHRYSTAL
Lieutenant General, USA
Director, Joint Staff

TABLE OF CONTENTS

APPENDIX

GLOSSARY

FIGURES

EXECUTIVE SUMMARY
COMMANDER'S OVERVIEW

- **Provides an Overview of Operational Contract Support and Key Terminology**
- **Lists Operational Contract Principals**
- **Lists Roles and Responsibilities for Operational Contract Support**
- **Discusses Contract Support Integration Planning and Execution**
- **Addresses the Details of Contractor Management**

Overview

The US military routinely uses contracted support in contingency operations.

The continual introduction of hi-tech equipment, coupled with force structure and manning reductions, and high operating tempo mean that military forces will often be significantly augmented with contracted support. To do this, contract support integration and contractor management must be integrated into military planning and operations. This is a complex and very challenging process.

Key terminology.

Commanders and their staffs must have a working knowledge of key joint contract support integration and contractor management related terms, since these terms are not widely known outside of the professional acquisition community.

Contingency acquisition, the process of acquiring supplies, services and construction in support of the joint operations begins at the point when a requiring activity identifies a specific requirement, defines the proper funding support, contract award, and administration requirement to satisfy activity needs.

Contract support is delivered to the joint force through a process comprised of five key tasks: planning; requirements determination;, contract development; contract execution; and contract closeout. The product of **planning** is a contract support integration plan that defines key contract support integration capabilities to include command and control (C2) relationships, boards and centers requirements, theater business clearance policies, etc. necessary to execute subordinate joint force commander (JFC) contract support integration requirements. Identifying, synchronizing, and prioritizing **requirements** are essential precursors to effective contract development, and essential to ensuring the subordinate JFC receives commercial support at the right place, at the right time, for the right price. The requirements process ends with a determination that the requirement is valid and of sufficient priority and that the requirement can only be met by commercial means. **Contract development** begins with the establishment of the proper contract venue as determined by the subordinate JFC and ends with contract award. **Contract execution** begins with the award of the contract by a warranted contracting officer and ends when contractor performance is complete or the contract is otherwise terminated by the contracting officer. **Contract closeout** is executed once the contract has been completed and all outstanding contract administration issues have been resolved and ends once the contracting officer has prepared a contract completion statement.

Planning encompasses all activities necessary to properly execute contract support integration requirements in an operational area.

Successful **operational contract support** is the ability to orchestrate and synchronize the provision of integrated contract support and management of contractor personnel providing that support to the joint force in a designated operational area.

Contingency contracting is the process of obtaining goods, services and construction from commercial sources via contracting means in support of contingency operations. It is a subset of contract support integration and does not include the requirements development, prioritization and budgeting processes. Contracts used in a contingency include theater support, systems support, and external support contracts.

Contract administration is a subset of contracting and includes efforts that ensure that supplies and services are delivered in accordance with the conditions and standards expressed in the contract. Contract administration is the oversight function, from contract award to contract close-out, performed by contracting professionals and designated noncontracting personnel.

Contractor management is closely related to, but not the same as, contract administration. Contractor management is a very expansive and complex process, which includes both the management of contractor performance and the management of the government's responsibilities for life and other support when such support is required by the JFC and has been incorporated into the terms and conditions of applicable contracts.

Types of contracted support.

It is important to understand the different types of contracts commonly used in support of contingency operations. **Theater support contracts** are contracts that are awarded by contracting officers in the operational area serving under the direct contracting authority of the Service component, special operations force command, or designated joint head of contracting activity (HCA) for the designated contingency operation. **Systems support contracts** are contracts awarded by Service acquisition program management offices that provide technical support, maintenance and, in some cases, repair parts for selected military weapon and support systems. Systems support contracts are routinely put in place to provide support to newly fielded weapons systems, including aircraft, land combat vehicles, and automated C2 systems. **External support contracts** are contracts awarded from contracting organizations whose contracting authority does not derive directly from the theater support contracting HCA(s) or from systems support contracting authorities. External support contracts provide a variety of logistic and other noncombat related services and supply support.

Key contracting personnel related terms.

Head of contracting activity is the official who has overall responsibility for managing the contracting activity. **Senior contracting official (SCO)** is a lead Service or joint command designated contracting official who has direct managerial responsibility over theater support contracting. **Contracting officer** is the government official with the legal authority to enter into, administer, and/or terminate contracts. **Contracting officer representative** is a Service member or Department of Defense (DOD) civilian designated and authorized in writing by a contracting officer who is to perform specific technical or administrative functions. **Field ordering officer** is a Service member or DOD civilian, who is appointed in writing and trained by a contracting officer, and authorized to execute micropurchases.

Contractor Personnel Related Terms. Contractors authorized to accompany the force (CAAF) are contingency contractor employees and all tiers of subcontractor employees who are specifically authorized through their contract to accompany the force and have protected status in accordance with international conventions. **Mission essential contractor employees** are defined as CAAF who are deemed by the contracting officer in consultation with the requiring activity as mission essential individuals. **Non-CAAF contractor employees** include local national (and third country national (TCN) expatriates who are permanent residents in the operational area) prime and associated subcontractor employees whose area of performance is not in the direct vicinity of US forces.

Other Important Related Terms. A prime contract is a contract or contractual action entered into by the US government (USG) for the purpose of obtaining supplies, materials, equipment, or services of any kind. **A subcontract** is a contract or contractual action entered into by a prime contractor, or subcontractor at any tier, for the purpose of obtaining supplies, materials, equipment, or services of any kind under a prime contract. **Privity of contract** is the legal relationship that exists between two contracting parties, for example, between the prime contractor and the United States. This fact can limit the ability of the JFC and subordinate commanders to directly enforce operational contract support policies on subcontractors and their personnel. **A performance work statement** is a statement of work for performance-based acquisitions that describes the required results in clear, specific, and objective terms with measurable outcomes. **An independent government estimate** is the government's estimate of the resources and projected cost of the resources a contractor will incur in the performance of the contract. **A requiring activity** is the military or other designated supported organization that identifies and receives contracted support during military operations. **The supported unit** is an organization that is the recipient of contractor-provided support. **An unauthorized commitment** is an agreement that is not binding on the government solely because the USG representative who made it lacked the authority to enter into that agreement on behalf of the USG. **Contract ratification** is the process of approving an unauthorized commitment by an official who has the authority to do so. **A constructive change to a contract** occurs when the contract work is actually changed but the terms and conditions of the contract have not been followed. Generally, a constructive change is an oral or written act or omission by an authorized government official that requires the contractor to perform work that is not a necessary part of the contract.

Principles and Processes

Operational Contract Support Principles.

Contracted support can be a significant force multiplier, but it is only one of numerous sources of support to the joint force.

Most joint operations will include significant contracted support.

Contracting is not just a source of logistic support; it can be used to acquire significant non-logistic support as well.

There are other non-cost related factors associated with contracted support that may not be readily apparent.

Contracted support and its associated contractor management challenges must be closely integrated early in the operation planning process.

Operational contract support can be a tremendous challenge during major operations and requires significant planning and management.

Contracting Principles. Contracted support differs significantly from military provided support. Contracted support relies on contract authority based in contract law, and the contract policies, processes, and procedures that support contract law.

Contracted support to military operations is administered in accordance with federal law and acquisition regulations.

Contracting authority does not equal command authority.

Multiple contracting authorities support (either directly or indirectly) any given contingency. Only warranted contracting officers have the authority to

obligate USG funds.

Care must be taken to avoid improper command influence on the contracting process.

Only a warranted contracting officer has the authority to make or change a contract.

Contracting requires centralized planning and decentralized execution to ensure effective, efficient use of limited local resources.

Contracting support can have a direct strategic impact on civil aspects of the operation.

Contractor Management Principles. While related to the contracting principles discussed above, contractor management principles are mainly focused on the integration of contractor personnel once the commander makes the decision to use contracted, vice military sources of support. **Contractor personnel are not a formal part of the military chain of command; (however, base and area** commanders do have limited directive authority over CAAF for matters of force protection (FP), security, safety, and general welfare of the force) therefore, Contractor personnel have a different legal status than military members and DOD civilians.

The **contractor management process** is composed of five key steps: planning, predeployment actions, deployment and reception, in-theater management, and redeployment. **Planning** for contractor personnel integration should be addressed in a separate contractor management plan appendix or in appropriate sections of operation plans (OPLANs) and operation orders (OPORDs). **Predeployment** actions include those actions taken by the government and the contract companies to ensure that CAAF are properly prepared to deploy in support of military operations. **Deployment and reception** involves managing the flow of CAAF into the designated joint operation area (JOA), including establishment of joint reception centers and procedures for contractor personnel entering the JOA. **In-theater management** involves orchestrating and managing the provision of day-to-day support to CAAF. **Redeployment** involves orchestrating the redeployment of the CAAF out of the designated JOA, once their period of performance ends.

Roles and Responsibilities

Understanding the roles and responsibilities of DOD, joint, and Service commanders and staffs related to operational contract support is critically important to all commands and staffs that may be involved with planning and managing contracted support and contractor management.

The Secretary of Defense (SecDef) is responsible for **issuing directives, instructions, and executing oversight** on the force apportionment process. **Under Secretary of Defense for Personnel and Readiness** is the primary staff assistant and advisor to SecDef for total force management and is responsible for policy, plans, and program development for the total force, which includes military, DOD civilian, and DOD contractor personnel. The **Under Secretary of Defense for Acquisition, Technology, and Logistics** serves as the Defense Acquisition Executive and has overall responsibility for the performance of the DOD Acquisition System, including establishing and publishing policies and procedures governing the operations of the DOD Acquisition System and the administrative oversight of defense contracts. **Deputy Under Secretary of Defense for Logistics and Material Readiness**, through the **Assistant Deputy Under Secretary of Defense (Program Support)**, is responsible for monitoring and managing the implementation of contractor management policy. **The Chairman of the Joint Chiefs of Staff (CJCS)**, as the **principal military advisor** to the President and the SecDef, has specific responsibilities in the areas of strategic direction as well as in strategic and contingency planning. **The Joint Staff Manpower and Personnel Directorate** establishes the manpower management, personnel support, and personnel service support policies and procedures for the total force during joint operations and administers oversight of joint personnel issues affecting the force. **The Joint Staff Intelligence Directorate** establishes procedures through joint doctrine for combatant commands to ensure proper vetting, for intelligence, counterintelligence, and FP purposes, of locally employed persons contracted by US forces to support US and coalition efforts. **The Joint Staff Operations Directorate** develops and provides guidance to the combatant commands regarding current operations and plans, including ensuring contracted support and associated contractor integration requirements are addressed in the Joint Operation Planning and Execution System policy and execution as well as providing the CJCS with recommended rules for the use of force by private security contractors and contractor personnel armed for personal protection, in support of joint operations. **The Joint Staff Logistics Directorate (J-4)** provides plans, policy, guidance, and oversight on joint logistics, including joint contingency operational contract support matters. **The Joint Staff Strategic Plans and Policy Directorate (J-5)** ensures operational contract support policies and procedures are included in–overarching policy documents to facilitate military operations. **The Joint Staff Command, Control, Communications, and Computers System Directorate (J-6)** provides advice and recommendations on information technology and national security systems matters for assessment of communications requirements in combatant command plans that require contracted support. **The Operational Plans and Joint Force Development Directorate (J-7),** through war plans, doctrine, education, training, exercises, concept development, capabilities-based planning, integrates contractor management related collective training requirements for Joint Chiefs of Staff exercises and joint professional military education programs. **The Joint Staff Legal Counsel** provides legal advice and guidance to the CJCS and other members of the Joint Staff and the combatant commands, as directed.

The Secretaries of the Military Departments provide administration and support of the forces assigned or attached to combatant commands, augmenting military support capabilities with contracted support when appropriate through their respective Service component commands assigned to the combatant commands. The Army, Marine Corps, Navy, and Air Force (under their respective Secretaries) are responsible for planning and executing contracting support to their own forces unless directed otherwise by a combatant commander.

Supported combatant commanders and subordinate JFCs, in determining and synchronizing contracted support requirements, contracting planning, as well as execution of operational contract support, work closely with the appropriate functional combatant commands, Service components, and DOD combat support agencies to determine operational contract support requirements, policies, and procedures.

DOD Agencies. The Defense Logistics Agency (DLA) is the DOD combat support agency responsible for providing effective and efficient worldwide logistics support to Military Departments and the combatant commands under conditions of peace and war. DLA also has its own contracting authority and can provide supply and service contracting during contingency operations. **Defense Contract Management Agency** is the combat support agency responsible for ensuring major DOD acquisition programs are delivered on time, within projected cost or price, and meet performance requirements. **Defense Contract Audit Agency (DCAA)** is a defense agency under the authority, direction, and control of the Under Secretary of Defense (Comptroller). DCAA is responsible for performing all contract audits for the DOD, and providing accounting and financial advisory services regarding contracts and subcontracts to all DOD components responsible for procurement and contract administration.

Contract Support Integration Planning and Execution

Contracting for supplies and services in support of military operations is a force multiplier.

Contracting is commonly used to augment organic military and other sources of support such as multinational logistic support, host-nation support, and to provide support where no organic capability exists, but contracting is often not properly planned for or integrated into the overall joint force logistic support effort.

Contracting authority is not the same as command authority.

Only the contracting officer has the authority to obligate the US government.

Contracting authority is the legal authority to enter into binding contracts and obligate funds for the USG, while command includes the authority and responsibility for effectively using available resources and for planning the employment of, organizing, directing, coordinating, and controlling military forces for the accomplishment of assigned missions. Contracting authority in the operational area flows from Congress to the President, then to the SecDef, through the Service/agency head, to the HCA, then to the SCO, and finally to the contracting officer. This contracting authority is explicitly documented via the contracting officer's warrant. **Command Authority** (combatant command [command authority]) includes the authority to perform functions involving organizing and employing commands and forces, assigning tasks and designating objectives, and giving authoritative direction over all aspects of an operation; it **does not include authority to make binding contracts or obligate funds on behalf of the USG.** Commanders at all levels must take care to avoid improper command influence, or its appearance, on the contracting process. The contracting officer must be able to independently exercise sound, unbiased business judgment and contract oversight in the accomplishment of the contracting mission. **The joint acquisition review board (JARB) is not a contracting board.** The JARB is utilized to coordinate and control the requirements generation and prioritization of joint common-user logistics (CUL) supplies and services that are needed in support of the operational mission and is normally chaired by the subordinate JFC (either subunified command or joint task force-level) or deputy commander or J-4. **The JARB's main role is to make specific approval and prioritization recommendations for all geographic combatant commander (GCC) directed, subordinate JFC controlled, high-value and/or high-visibility CUL requirements and to include recommendations on the proper source of support for these requirements.** The joint contracting support board (JCSB) reviews contract support requirement forwarded by_the JARB and makes recommendations on which specific contracting organizations/contract venues are best suited to fulfill the requirements. **The goal of the JCSB is to maximize the contracting capabilities of the JOA while minimizing the competition for limited vendor capabilities.**

Much of a Service component's equipment will be maintained either partially or fully through contracted logistic support.

Systems support contracts are generally issued when the Service systems contracting activities award the original systems contracts. Because such support is generally awarded long before and unrelated to a particular deployment requirement and is codified into the contract through generic deployment support language or clauses, the **GCC and subordinate JFC must be cognizant of the impact of overly restrictive CAAF theater entrance requirements and/or contracted support use restrictions on readiness of key weapon and support systems deployed to the theater.** The JFC's main concern with the use of systems support contracts in military operations has to do with contractor personnel management related issues.

External support contracts are often used to provide significant logistic support and selected non-logistic support to the joint force. Like systems support contracts, external support contracting authority does not come as a direct result of the contingency operation. Generally, these contracts are issued during peacetime for use during contingencies. It is important to understand that these civil augmentation program and other external support contracts remain under the control of the Service components and do not normally fall under the authority of the GCC operational contract support.

Theater support contracts are those contracts that are issued by deployed contingency contracting officers and are generally awarded to local vendors to support in-theater customers. This type of support contracting can be used to acquire support from commercial sources similar to those external support contract services and/or can be used to acquire limited amounts of commercially available supply items from both local and global sources. Theater support contracts are those contracts that are most commonly referred to as contingency contracts.

There is no single preferred contracting organizational option.

Contracting Support Organizational Options. There are three main contracting related organizational options: Service component support to own forces; lead Service; and joint theater support contracting command. The specific organizational option that is exercised is determined by the GCC in coordination with the subordinate JFC and Service components and is chosen entirely dependent on the mission requirements and operational factors. Just as there is no one preferred option, the needs of the contracting organization may change as the operation progresses. Therefore, the contracting organizational structure may change and/or progress through the basic organizational options as the organizational needs unfold. During smaller scale operations with an expected short duration, the GCC would normally choose the **Service component support to own forces** option, allowing the Service component commanders to retain control of their own theater support contracting authority and organizations. **The lead Service** organizational option is most appropriate for major, long-term operations where the supported GCC and subordinate JFC desire to ensure that there is a consolidated contracting effort within the operational area, but without the need to stand-up an entirely new joint command. In larger or more complex contingency operations, the supported GCC may require more oversight than what can typically be provided through the lead Service organizational option. In this case, the **joint theater support contracting command**

organizational option would likely be the most appropriate.

The use of contracted support must be addressed early in the planning cycle.

Contract Support Integration Planning and Execution. In all operations where there will be a significant use of contracted support, the supported GCC and their subordinate commanders and staffs must ensure that this support is properly addressed in the appropriate OPLAN/OPORD. Accordingly, a contractor support integration plan (CSIP) is developed by the logistics staff contracting personnel, assisted by the lead Service (if a lead Service is designated). Additionally, each Service component should publish its own CSIP seeking integration and unity of effort within the supported GCC's CSIP.

Contracting Support by Phase of the Operation. As the operation progresses, contracting support will generally shift based on the operational phase: mobilization; initial deployment; joint reception, staging, onward movement, and integration; employment sustainment; and finally, redeployment. These stages of contracting support are generally characterized by the types of items purchased and the types of contracting mechanisms used to support specific force support requirements.

Other Key Contracting Planning and Execution Considerations. There are numerous other contracting planning and execution considerations that must be taken into account by the supported GCC, subordinate JFC, and Service components. These considerations run the gamut from contracting support to multinational operations to support of major interagency-led reconstruction requirements, as well as media and political visibility of decisions about selection of contractors and the actions of contractors once in the operational area.

Contractor Management

The management and control of contractor personnel is significantly different than command and control of military members.

Unlike military members and DOD civilians, contractor personnel are not part of the direct chain-of-command. They are managed and controlled through contractor management and governmental oversight staff in accordance with terms and conditions of their contract. **Commanders do not generally have legal authority to direct contractor personnel to perform tasks outside of their contract**; however, in emergency situations, the ranking area or base commander may direct contractors authorized to accompany the force to take FP or emergency response actions not specifically authorized in their contract as long as those actions do not require them to assume inherently governmental responsibilities. While the management and control aspect is unique to this category of the "total force," there are numerous additional risks and challenges that must be dealt with when utilizing contracted vice military support.

Contractor personnel management is accomplished through a myriad of different requiring activities, contracting officer representatives (CORs), supported units, contracting organizations, and contractor company management personnel, many of which are not under direct JFC C2. Key to success in this contractor personnel management challenge is for the GCC and subordinate JFCs to establish clear, enforceable, and well understood contractor theater entrance, accountability, FP, and general contractor management policies and procedures early in the planning stages of any military contingency. The military chain of command exercises management control over contractor personnel through the contract management team, consisting of the contracting officer, COR, and the "on-site" contract company manager.

Contractor Personnel Legal Status and Discipline. Law of war treaties attempt to establish and clarify the status of contractors when supporting military operations. These treaties entitle CAAF to be treated as POWs. CAAF are contractor employees who are specifically authorized through their contract to accompany the force and have protected legal status IAW international conventions. IAW these international conventions, **CAAF are non-combatants, but are entitled to prisoner of war (POW) status if detained.** On the other hand, **Non-CAAF employees** (employees of commercial entities not authorized CAAF status but who are under contract to DOD) have no special legal status IAW international conventions or agreements and are legally considered civilians. They may not receive Geneva conventions identification cards, thus **are not entitled to POW treatment if captured** by forces observing applicable international law. Legal jurisdiction and commander's authority over contractor personnel varies depending on contractor personnel nationality, CAAF or non-CAAF designations, operational specific policies, and the type and severity of the discipline infraction. Normally, local national contract employees are subject to local and/or HN laws while

US citizens and TCN CAAF may or may not be subject to local and/or HN laws. **All CAAF however, are subject to US federal law.**

Deployment/Redeployment Planning and Preparation. Contractor management planning is related to, but not the same as, contracting support integration planning. While the CSIP is focused on how DOD will acquire and manage contracted support, contractor management planning is focused on the government obligations under the terms and conditions of the contract to provide support to contractor personnel. There is no single primary or special staff officer responsible to lead the contractor management planning effort. To address this situation, the JFC should consider establishing a contractor personnel integration working group to ensure the various contractor integration challenges are addressed and integrated across all primary and special staff lines.

FP and security of contractor personnel and equipment is a shared responsibility between the contractor and the government. In a permissive environment, the supported GCC and subordinate JFC may have only limited special planning considerations and this security responsibility would normally fall to the contractor. In general, military provided FP is the preferred option for operations where there is an on-going or anticipated level II threat (small-scale, irregular forces conducting unconventional war) or level III threat (conventional forces capable of air, land, or sea attacks). The contracting officer shall include in the contract the level of protection to be provided to contingency contractor personnel. All contingency contractor personnel whose area of performance is in the vicinity of US forces shall be required to comply with applicable supported GCC and subordinate JFC FP policies and procedures. The JFC and individual base commanders are responsible for the security of all military facilities within the operational area. Not having these policies and procedures in place can severely reduce the effectiveness, timeliness, flexibility, and/or efficiency of contracted support. This can be an especially significant issue when changes to the operation require a quick surge of contracted support from one base to another.

Government Provided Support. As most military operations are conducted in austere and/or hostile and uncertain environments, contractor personnel support will often be provided through military means or via another contract directed by the military. In these situations, the contracting officer will detail the government support to be provided in the terms and conditions of the contract, after determining support requirements and availability of such support from theater DOD support providers.

Coordinating Non DOD Contract Support. The scope of non-DOD contract support integration requirements are very much mission dependent. In some joint operations, the JFC may have only limited requirements to integrate non-DOD contracted support into military operations while in others, there may be major challenges that defy any simple solution. In complex, long-term stability operations, there are a myriad of challenges related to other government agency, intergovernmental organization, and nongovernmental organization contractors. Key to addressing these requirements is an active civil-military coordination effort to include the use of civil-military operations centers or other mechanisms to ensure proper civil-military information sharing and cooperation.

CONCLUSION

This publication establishes doctrine for planning, conducting, and assessing contracting and contractor management functions in support of joint operations. It provides standardized guidance and information related to integrating operational contract support and contractor management, defines and describes these two different, but directly related functions, and provides a basic discussion on contracting C2 organizational options.

Intentionally Blank

CHAPTER I
INTRODUCTION

> *"The Department's Total Force – its active and reserve military components, its civil servants, and its contractors – constitutes its warfighting capability and capacity."*
>
> **Department of Defense Quadrennial Defense Review, 2006**

1. General

a. The US military routinely uses contracted support in contingency operations. The continual introduction of hi-tech equipment, coupled with force structure and manning reductions, and high operating tempo mean that military forces will often be significantly augmented with contracted support. Accordingly, the supported geographic combatant commander (GCC), subordinate joint force commanders (JFCs), and their staffs must be familiar with how to plan for and integrate contracted support to joint operations.

> **CONTRACTING SUPPORT IN WORLD WAR II**
>
> **At the beginning of World War II, over 1,000 civilian construction workers were employed by the US Navy to expand the airfield on Wake Island. During the actual battle, many of these contractor personnel provided direct support to the Marines by performing tasks such as litter bearer, delivering ammunition, etc. Some actually picked up weapons and took a direct part in the fight. Of the 1,014 contractor personnel taken prisoner after the battle, approximately 16% (~180) died during their captivity, including 98 who were executed on Wake Island in October of 1943.**
>
> **SOURCE: *The Defense of Wake,* USMC Historical Monograph**

b. Integrating the two related, but different, operational contact support constructs of contract support integration and contractor management functions into military planning and operations is a complex and very challenging process. Multiple joint and Service component organizations are involved in this process, including commanders and their staffs at the combatant command through major tactical force levels. Additionally, numerous contracting organizations from both inside and outside of the operational area play a vital role in operational contract support planning and execution. Finally, the development of the Joint Operation Planning and Execution System (JOPES) annex W at the combatant command and subordinate command levels, along with supporting Service component plans, crosses primary and special staff lanes, yet, these staffs are generally unfamiliar with the contract support integration process and associated contractor management challenges.

2. Key Terminology Discussion

a. **General Contracting Related Terms and Related Discussion Points.** It is very important that commanders and their staffs have a working knowledge of the key contract support integration and contractor management related terms discussed below. Since these terms are not widely known outside of the professional acquisition community, a discussion is provided here. Without a basic understanding of these terms, effective planning and execution of this complex source of support is more difficult.

IMPORTANT NOTE

Many of the terms discussed below are found in the Federal Acquisition Regulation and Department of Defense Federal Acquisition Regulation Supplement; however, some of the actual doctrine definitions established in JP 4-10 have been modified from the regulatory definition to meet joint doctrine administrative guidelines. In no case has the actual meaning of the term been changed.

(1) **Contingency acquisition** is the process of acquiring supplies, services, and construction in support of the operations. Acquisition includes obtaining support from multiple sources to include: multinational military capabilities, host-nation support (HNS), or contracted support. From the contracting aspect, contingency acquisition begins at the point when a requiring activity identifies a specific requirement and defines the requirement to the level necessary to satisfy activity needs, which includes proper funding support, contract award, and administration. This joint publication will address the overall acquisition process only as it applies to contracting.

(2) **Operational contract support** is the process of planning for and obtaining supplies, services, and construction from commercial sources in support of joint operations along with the associated contractor management functions. Successful operational contract support is the ability to orchestrate and synchronize the provision of integrated contracted support and management of contractor personnel providing that support to the joint force in a designated operational area. Contract support integration is the coordination and synchronization of contracted support executed in a designated operational area in support of the joint force. Contractor management is the oversight and integration of contractor personnel and associated equipment providing that support to the joint force in a designated operational area. While directly related, contract support integration and contractor management are not one-and-the same and both require significant JFC oversight.

(3) **Contingency contracting** is the process of obtaining supplies, services, and construction from commercial sources via contracting means in support of contingency operations. Contingency contracting is a subset of contract support integration and does not include the requirements development, prioritization, and budgeting processes. Additionally, contingency contracting does not encompass special methods for procuring supplies, services, and minor construction that result from special authorizations that allow for acquisition actions outside of generally established procurement rules. Contingency contracting, by definition, is conducted by contracting officers warranted under authorities granted to the Services and other components under Title 10, United States Code (USC) in accordance with (IAW) rules established in the Federal Acquisition Regulation (FAR), Defense Federal Acquisition Regulation Supplement (DFARS), Service FAR supplements

(Title 48, Code of Federal Regulations [CFR]), and applicable contingency contracting acquisition instructions.

(4) A **contingency contract** is a legally binding agreement for supplies, services, and construction let by government contracting officers in the operational area as well as other contracts that have a prescribed area of performance within a designated operational area. Contracts used in a contingency include theater support, systems support, and external support contracts described below.

(5) **Contract administration** is a subset of contracting and includes efforts that ensure that supplies, services, and construction are delivered IAW the conditions and standards expressed in the contract. Contract administration is the oversight function, from contract award to contract close-out, performed by contracting professionals and designated noncontracting personnel. It includes ensuring that both parties (government and contractor) meet the specified terms and conditions of the contract. Contract administration is composed of 70 functions, as described in FAR Part 42, including monitoring contract compliance, performing property administration, and performing quality assurance. Contract administration conducted during contingency operations is referred to as contingency contract administration services (CCAS).

(6) **Contractor management** is the ability to manage and maintain visibility of contractor personnel and associated contractor equipment providing support to the joint force in a designated operational area. It is closely related to, but not the same as, contract administration. Contractor management is a very expansive and complex process. Contractor management includes both the management of contractor performance in complying with contractor personnel related requirements and the management of the government's responsibilities for life and other support when such support is required by the JFC and has been incorporated into the terms and conditions of applicable contracts. Contractor management includes those activities necessary to deploy, receive, manage, and redeploy contractor personnel, especially as described in Department of Defense Instruction (DODI) 3020.41, *Contractor Personnel Authorized to Accompany the US Armed Forces,* and its associated references.

b. **Types of Contracted Support.** It is important to understand the different types of contracts commonly used in support of contingency operations. This construct breaks support contracts into three categories describing the numerous contracting and contract administration authorities providing support within the operational area. It outlines the limits on the JFC's ability to control/influence these different types of contracted support.

(1) **Theater support contracts** are contracts that are awarded by contracting officers in the operational area serving under the direct contracting authority of the Service component, special operations force command, or designated joint head of contracting activity (HCA) for the designated contingency operation. During a contingency, these contracts are normally executed under expedited contracting authority and provide supplies, services, and construction from commercial sources generally within the operational area. **Theater support contracts are the type of contract typically associated with the term**

contingency contracting. Also of importance from the contractor management perspective is that local national personnel make up the bulk of the theater support contract employees.

(2) **Systems support contracts** are contracts awarded by a Military Department acquisition program management (PM) offices that provide technical support, maintenance and, in some cases, repair parts for selected military weapon and support systems. Systems support contracts are routinely put in place to provide support to newly fielded weapons systems, including aircraft, land combat vehicles, and automated C2 systems. Systems support contracting authority, contract management, and program management authority resides with the Military Department systems materiel acquisition program offices. Systems support contractor employees, made up mostly of US citizens, provide support in garrison and often deploy with the force in both training and contingency operations.

(3) **External support contracts** are contracts awarded by contracting organizations whose contracting authority does not derive directly from the theater support contracting HCA(s) or from systems support contracting authorities. External support contracts provide a variety of logistic and other noncombat related services and supply support. Some examples of external support contracts are the Services' civil augmentation program (CAP) contracts including the Army's Logistics Civil Augmentation Program (LOGCAP), the Air Force Contract Augmentation Program (AFCAP), the Navy's Global Contingency Construction Contract (GCCC) and Global Contingency Service Contract (GCSC), Defense Logistics Agency (DLA) prime vendor contracts, and Navy fleet husbanding contracts. External support contracts normally include a mix of US citizens, third country nationals (TCNs), and local national contractor employees.

c. **Key Contracting Personnel Related Terms.** Understanding key contracting personnel positions and their authority is very important in planning and coordinating contracted support for military operations.

(1) **Head of contracting activity** is the official who has overall responsibility for managing the contracting activity. HCAs do not typically exercise command authority within the operational area. **There are multiple HCAs across multiple military organizations and types of contracted support utilized in joint operations.** Contracting authority flows from the Services, United States Special Operations Command (USSOCOM), United States Transportation Command (USTRANSCOM), and combat support agencies through designated HCAs to their contracting officers.

(2) **Senior contracting official (SCO)** is a lead Service or joint command designated contracting official who has direct managerial responsibility over theater support contracting. There may be multiple SCOs in the same operational area based on mission or regional focus. For example, at one time in Operation IRAQI FREEDOM (OIF), there were two SCOs (known as the principal assistant responsible for contracting or PARC), one for support to forces and one for reconstruction support.

(3) **Contracting officer** is the government official (uniformed or civilian) with the legal authority to enter into, administer, and/or terminate contracts. Within all components,

the contracting officer is appointed in writing through a warrant (Standard Form [SF] 1402) by the HCA or the SCO. **Only duly warranted contracting officers are authorized to obligate the US government (USG), legally binding it to make payments against contracts. Active and Reserve Component military officers and enlisted members, as well as Department of Defense (DOD) civilian personnel, may serve as contracting officers supporting deployed joint forces.** The three main types of contracting officers are procuring contracting officers (PCOs), administrative contracting officers (ACOs), and terminating contracting officers. Unlike PCOs, ACOs duties are limited to administering the contract.

(4) **Contracting officer representative** is a Service member or DOD civilian designated and authorized in writing by a contracting officer who is to perform specific technical or administrative functions. The COR is normally assigned to the requiring unit or activity and may serve in this COR position as a collateral or extra duty. COR primary duties may include monitoring contractor performance, providing quality assurance, certifying receipt of services, and acting as a liaison between the requiring activity and the contracting officer. While CORs require formal training and certification, **they do not have authority to change, add to, or otherwise modify a contract.**

(5) **Field ordering officer (FOO)** is a Service member or DOD civilian, who is appointed in writing and trained by a contracting officer. FOOs are authorized by the contracting officer to execute micropurchases using the SF 44 up to a designated threshold in support of forces and/or designated civil-military operations. FOOs are not warranted contracting officers and their FOO duties are considered an extra or collateral duty. Not all Services use FOOs in support of military operations.

d. **Contractor Personnel Related Terms.** These contractor personnel related terms are based in customary international law and DOD policy. These definitions are very important when it comes to understanding the legal status of the contractor employees as well as determining government furnished support requirements. DODI 3020.41, *Contractor Personnel Authorized to Accompany the US Armed Forces*, codifies these terms within DOD policy.

(1) **Contractors authorized to accompany the force (CAAF)** are contingency contractor employees and all tiers of subcontractor employees who are specifically authorized through their contract to accompany the force and have protected status IAW international conventions. Generally, all US citizens and TCN contingency contractor and subcontractor employees who do not normally reside within the operational area, whose area of performance is in the direct vicinity of US forces, and who routinely reside with US forces (especially in uncertain or hostile environments) are considered CAAF. CAAF also may include some mission essential local national contractor employees (e.g., interpreters) who reside with US forces and receive government furnished support such as billeting and access to dining facilities. All CAAF will be subject to individual personnel accountability standards; are required to meet specified deployment preparation requirements; and will be provided requisite government furnished support as identified in the contract. However, US citizens, as well as selected mission essential TCN and local national CAAF, may receive a

higher level of government furnished support in areas such as force protection (FP), personnel recovery (PR), access to postal service, etc. CAAF support is discussed in detail in Chapter IV, "Contractor Management."

(2) **Mission essential contractor employees** are defined as CAAF who are deemed by the contracting officer in consultation with the requiring activity as mission essential individuals. Mission essential CAAF have managerial or technical skills not commonly found in the general population. Examples of mission essential CAAF include, but are not limited to: CAP contractor managers, systems support contract field service representatives (FSRs), and interpreters.

(3) **Non-CAAF** include local national (and TCN expatriates who are permanent residents in the operational area) prime and associated subcontractor employees whose area of performance is not in the direct vicinity of US forces. Non-CAAF also include nonmission essential personnel (e.g., day laborers, delivery personnel, and cleaning service personnel) who do not reside with US forces nor receive government furnished support such as billeting and subsistence. Government furnished support requirements of non-CAAF are typically limited to FP and emergency medical care when performing their jobs in the direct vicinity of US forces.

e. **Other Important Related Terms**. The following terms and discussion will help provide a frame of reference to the JFC and subordinate commanders to better understand the challenges and responsibilities related to contract support integration.

(1) **A prime contract** is a contract or contractual action entered into by the USG for the purpose of obtaining supplies, materials, equipment, or services of any kind. The prime contractor is the organization that has entered into a prime contract with the United States. The United States has privity of contract only with the prime contractor.

(2) **A subcontract** is a contract or contractual action entered into by a prime contractor, or subcontractor at any tier, for the purpose of obtaining supplies, materials, equipment, or services of any kind under a prime contract. The prime contractor is responsible for the actions of the direct subcontractor. Likewise, subcontractors are responsible for managing any subcontractor at the next lower tier. Subcontractors and their employees should be treated the same as the prime contractor when it comes to contractor management planning and actions.

(3) **Privity of contract** is the legal relationship that exists between two contracting parties, for example, between the prime contractor and the United States. This term is important to the JFC in that only the prime contractor has direct responsibility to the government. This fact can limit the ability of the JFC and subordinate commanders to directly enforce operational contract support policies on subcontractors and their personnel although flow-down provisions for such policies require contractors to enforce such policies on lower-tier subcontractors when compliance with such policies is included in the terms and conditions of the contract.

(4) **A performance work statement (PWS)** is a statement of work (SOW) for performance-based acquisitions that describes the required results in clear, specific, and objective terms with measurable outcomes. While contracting personnel may be able to provide guidance, templates, or information on previous like-purchases, PWS development is the responsibility of the requiring activity.

(5) **An independent government estimate (IGE)** is the government's estimate of the resources and projected cost of the resources a contractor will incur in the performance of the contract. These costs include direct costs such as labor, supplies, equipment, or transportation and indirect costs such as labor overhead, material overhead, as well as general and administrative expenses, profit, or fee. The IGE is prepared by government personnel (i.e., not the contractor that will provide the goods/services). While contracting personnel may be able to provide guidance, templates, or information on previous like-purchases; IGE development is the responsibility of the requiring activity.

(6) **A requiring activity** is the military or other designated supported organization that identifies the requirement and receives contracted support during military operations. The requiring activity has specific responsibilities in the contracting and contractor management process to include ensuring that there is proper contractor management oversight assistance provided through an appointed unit COR. Other requiring activity responsibilities include conducting initial research on available commercial sources of support, developing the IGE, drafting the initial PWS, and obtaining proper funding.

See Appendix G, "Requirements Development and Acquisition Review Processes," *for more information on requiring activity responsibilities.*

(7) **The supported unit** is an organization that is the recipient of contractor-provided support. A supported unit may also be the requiring activity, if it initiates the request for support. **In some cases, such as with CAP support, the supported unit may not be the requiring activity such as when a lead Military Department is directed to provide common-user logistics (CUL) support to the entire joint force.** Even when not officially the requiring activity, supported units play an important role in assisting the JFC and Service component commanders and may be required to provide a COR to assist the requiring activity and a contracting officer to monitor this contracted support. In almost all situations, the supported unit, will at a minimum, play a role in integrating selected contractor personnel into local military operations.

(8) **An unauthorized commitment** is an agreement that is not binding on the government solely because the USG representative who made it lacked the authority to enter into that agreement on behalf of the USG. **It is important for the JFC and subordinate commanders and staff personnel to understand that only warranted contracting officers are authorized to enter into contractual agreements or to modify existing contracts.** USG officials (both military members and civilians) can be held pecuniarily liable for unauthorized commitments depending on the circumstances and conduct of the individual.

(9) **Contract ratification** is the process of approving an unauthorized commitment by an official who has the authority to do so. Ratification is never automatic; and even when ratification is possible, commanders are required to take corrective administrative action against the individuals causing the unauthorized commitment. Corrective actions may include official reprimands or other disciplinary action commanders deem appropriate. If the transaction cannot be ratified, the individual who committed the transaction may be personally responsible for the debt and may be subject to litigation by the company to recover the price of the transaction.

(10) **A constructive change to a contract** occurs when the contract work is actually changed outside the terms and conditions of the contract. Generally, a constructive change is an oral or written act or omission by an authorized government official that requires the contractor to perform work that is not a necessary part of the contract, usually at a higher cost. This is something that differs from advice, comments, suggestions, or opinions, which government engineering or technical personnel frequently offer to a contractor's employees.

3. Operational Contract Support Principles

Planning for and integrating contracted support into military operations is dependent on various factors and represents a tremendous challenge for the supported GCC, subordinate JFCs, and Service component commanders. C2 of contracting organizations and contractor management are special challenges for the JFC. The following discussion provides overarching principles that are important to understanding these challenges. JOPES provides the planning templates and supporting information systems required for thorough operational contract support plan development and integration.

a. **General Principles.** The following principles apply to all aspects of planning and managing contracted support.

(1) **Contracted support can be a significant force multiplier, but it is only one of numerous sources of support to the joint force.** The supported GCC and JFCs must judiciously consider the proper mix of different sources of support to include: US military support, multinational military support, HNS, and contracting support. Each of these sources of support has advantages and disadvantages that must be carefully weighed by the JFC and subordinate Service component commanders.

(2) **Most joint operations will include significant contracted support.** While some limited duration operations such as noncombatant evacuation operations, may utilize limited contracted support, all major operations will involve significant contracted support. This is especially true for major, long-term stability operations.

(3) **Contracting is not just a source of logistic support; it can be used to acquire significant non-logistic support as well.** Contracting is often used to acquire support well beyond logistics. Contracted support can include significant support capabilities such as interpreter support, interrogation support, signal support, etc.

(4) **There are other non-cost related factors associated with contracted support that may not be readily apparent.** These factors include but are not limited to: inability to assign collateral/extra duties; compliance with the terms and conditions of the contract; inability to direct contractor on "how to do a task"; time delays for performance when work changes and contract modifications are required; contract oversight responsibilities by CORs; security escort responsibilities; and potential effects on morale when contractor working/living conditions differ from. These factors should be carefully weighed when considering contracting for support.

(5) **Contracted support and its associated contractor management challenges must be closely integrated early in the operation planning process.** Contracted support is a force multiplier for the joint force. However, it is complex and comes with costs that often may not be apparent to the military, especially in terms of managing the associated contractor personnel and providing government furnished support to them. Proper planning will better integrate the contractor force into military operations and mitigate unplanned burdens on the joint force. The importance of such integrated planning cannot be overemphasized.

(6) **Operational contract support can be a tremendous challenge during major operations and requires significant planning and management.** These management processes require proper planning and adequate personnel resources. These processes also require visibility of contracts and contractor personnel, both of which can be very difficult to obtain and maintain in large, fast-paced operations.

b. **Contract Support Integration Principles.** Contracted support differs significantly from military provided support. Contracted support relies on contract authority based in contract law, and the contract policies, processes, and procedures that support contract law. These policies, processes, and procedures represent special support conditions and limitations that must be articulated in planning and followed in plan execution. Contracted support to a joint force results from efforts and interactions of a myriad of players including requiring activities, finance organizations, and contracting activities. In a large contingency, contracted support of the joint force can emanate from requirements brought forth by numerous requiring activities through contracts let under the authority of multiple Military Departments, defense agency, USSOCOM, and USTRANSCOM HCAs from both inside and outside the operational area. The complexity and special considerations associated with the flow of this support makes it mandatory that supported units from the combatant command down to the tactical-level not only understand and comply with these legally mandated contract authorities but also have a basic understanding of the types of contracts that provide support and the associated processes that deliver this contracted support to the joint force. A brief summary follows:

Chapter III, "Contract Support Integration," *covers these principles in depth.*

(1) **Contracted support to military operations is administered IAW federal law and acquisition regulations.** Contracting support must be administered IAW US public law along with the FAR, DFARS, and Military Department FAR supplements. FAR

Part 18 and DFARS Part 218 outline emergency procurement authorities that may be available during contingency operations. These contract law emergency authorities must be considered, and requested as necessary, based on GCC and/or subordinate JFC planning efforts.

(2) **Contracting authority does not equal command authority.** Command authority is the legal authority of the commander to organize and employ assigned and attached forces; however, **this command authority does not include the authority to make binding contracts for the USG**. Only warranted contracting officers have this authority, which flows from the Military Departments, USTRANSCOM, USSOCOM, and select DOD agencies and activities through designated HCAs.

(3) **Multiple contracting authorities support (either directly or indirectly) any given contingency.** In most situations, the JFC will have limited direct control over external support contracts and very little influence over decisions related to the use of systems support contracts. However, all subordinate commanders should be aware of combatant commander (CCDR) or JFC guidance on contracting requirements for their operational area.

Additional options for contracting organizations are discussed in Chapter III, "Contract Support Integration."

(4) **Only warranted contracting officers have the authority to obligate the USG.** This authority, derived from the US Constitution, federal law, and the FAR, is documented in the contracting officer's warrant.

(5) **Care must be taken to avoid improper command influence on the contracting process.** Commanders should take great care to avoid improper influence over the contracting process and subordinate contracting organizations. Such improper influence may result in fraud, waste, and abuse of precious contract resources and dollars.

(6) **Only a warranted contracting officer has the authority to make or change a contract.** Commanders, government civilians, and other non-warranted military members need to understand that they can incur pecuniary liability for unauthorized commitments and are subject to disciplinary actions depending on the circumstances.

(7) **Contracting requires centralized planning and decentralized execution to ensure effective, efficient use of limited local resources.** In many operations, multiple theater support and external support contracting activities may be competing for the same locally available commercial vendor base - thereby dramatically inflating cost to the detriment of the joint force operation. It is very important that the supported GCC and subordinate JFCs develop adequate plans and policies to ensure visibility of all contract requirements and associated contracts, available for execution within the operational area. The GCC and subordinate JFC also must be prepared to deconflict these requirements based on the recommendations of specific contracting related boards and requisite command/coordination guidance in the appropriate orders and directives.

(8) **Contracted support can have a direct strategic impact on civil aspects of the operation.** While the most important factor of contracted support is effectiveness of support to the military force, in certain operations the JFC may choose to utilize theater support and some external support contracts to also provide a positive economic and social impact on the local populace. Tying the contracting effort directly to the civil-military aspects of the JFC's plan requires very close coordination between the lead contracting activity, normally a lead Service or joint theater support contracting command, and the JFC plans and operations staff. This effort can be especially important in counterinsurgency or long-term stability operations.

(9) **There are some functions considered inherently governmental that should not be contracted.** Most combat support and sustainment functions can be partially or fully contracted. Some specific functions are deemed inherently governmental and may not be performed by contractors. These include combat operations, contract award, and supervision of military members and DOD civilians.

IAW the FAR, "inherently governmental function" means, as a matter of policy, a function that is so intimately related to the public interest as to mandate performance by government employees. More detailed information on inherently governmental functions can be found in DODI 1100.22, Guidance for Determining Workforce Mix.

c. **Contract Support Integration Process.** Contracted support is delivered to the joint force through a process comprised of five key tasks: planning; requirements determination; contract development; contract execution; and contract closeout.

(1) **Planning encompasses** all activities necessary to properly execute contract support integration requirements in an operational area. The product of this task is a contract support integration plan (CSIP), which defines key contract support integration capabilities to include command and control (C2) relationships, boards and centers requirements, theater business clearance policies, etc., necessary to execute subordinate JFC contract support integration requirements. It is crucial that supported units from the combatant command down to the tactical-level have a basic understanding of the key considerations and processes associated with integrating contractor personnel and equipment into the joint force. Successful contractor management results from efforts and interactions of a myriad of players including requiring activities, contracting activities, various staff officers from the GCC, subordinate JFC, and Service components.

(2) **Requirements determination** encompasses all activities necessary to define, vet, and prioritize joint force requirements. Effective contract support is driven primarily by timely and accurate requirements. Identifying, synchronizing, and prioritizing requirements are essential precursors to effective contract development, and essential to ensuring the subordinate JFC receives commercial support at the right place, at the right time, and the right price. Requirements determination is a command, not contracting, function. While guided by the CSIP, requiring activities are responsible to develop a clear description of the requirement, perform market research, obtain appropriate approvals, and ensure adequate funding is available. The requirements process ends with a determination that the

requirement is valid and of sufficient priority and that the requirement can only be met by commercial means.

(3) **Contract development** begins with the establishment of the proper contract venue as determined by the subordinate JFC. Depending on the contract type and dollar amount, this step may include development of a formal solicitation package, a pre-business clearance, legal review, and submission for formal advertising of the solicitation to the contractor community and negotiations. This step ends with contract award.

(4) **Contract execution** begins with the award of the contract by a warranted contracting officer. This step includes monitoring of contract performance and execution of contract modifications by the contracting officer and for all service contracts, designation of requiring activity nominated contracting officer representatives (CORs), and, when required, post-award changes to the contract (contract modifications). Contract execution ends when contractor performance is complete or the contract is otherwise terminated by the contracting officer.

(5) **Contract closeout** is executed once the contract has been completed and all outstanding contract administration issues have been resolved. This step includes initiating final payment to and/or collection from the contractor, de-obligating excess funds, and finalizing records disposal/disposition. Contract closeout ends once the contracting officer has prepared a contract completion statement and places a signed original in the contract file.

d. **Contractor Management Principles.** While related to the contract support integration principles discussed above, contractor management principles are mainly focused on the integration of contractor personnel once the commander makes the decision to use contracted, vice military, sources of support.

Chapter IV, "Contractor Management" *covers these contractor principles in depth.*

(1) **Contractor personnel are not a formal part of the military chain of command; however** base and area commanders do have limited directive authority over CAAF for matters of FP, security, safety, and general welfare of the force. Commanders also have limited legal jurisdiction over CAAF as described in Chapter IV, "Contractor Management." Outside of this directive authority for tactical matters and limited legal jurisdiction, individual contractor employees are managed by contractor personnel supervisors and through established government contracting management channels IAW the terms and conditions of their contract.

(2) **Contractor personnel have a different legal status than military members and DOD civilians**. IAW recognized international agreements, contractor personnel identified as CAAF must be identified as such through the issuance of an appropriate identification (ID) card and letter of authorization (LOA); however, unlike other noncombatants, they should be afforded prisoner of war (POW) status when detained.

(3) **Discipline and Commander's Authority Challenges.** Legal jurisdiction and commander's authority over contractor personnel varies depending on contractor personnel nationality, CAAF or non-CAAF designations, operational specific policies, and the type and severity of the discipline infraction. Commanders and legal staffs at all levels need to be aware of current US law, DOD policy, and local directives related to contractor personnel discipline and commander's authority related to CAAF and any non-CAAF contractor employee who requires temporary access to military facilities.

(4) **"Other duties as assigned" is not relevant to contractor personnel.** Because contractor personnel are managed IAW their contract, they cannot be ordered to perform functions that are outside the scope of their contract. This can cause a lack of flexibility to the tactical-level commander when compared to utilizing military members for the same support function.

(5) **Contractor management planning and procedures cross most primary and special staff functional lanes.** Contractor management integration requirements run the gamut from establishing specific contractor personnel theater entrance standards to integrating contractor personnel into the local security programs. Detailed planning and mission specific contractor management procedural guidance is not the primary responsibility of the contracting officers or logistics staffs. The staff officer for each specific functional requirement (e.g., manpower and personnel directorate of a joint staff [J-1] for personnel service support, joint force surgeon for health service support requirements, operations directorate of a joint staff [J-3] for FP requirements) has overall responsibility for their specific portion of contractor management planning and execution.

e. **Contractor Management Process.** The contractor management process is composed of five key steps: planning, predeployment actions, deployment and reception, in-theater management, and redeployment.

(1) **Planning** for contractor personnel integration should be addressed in a separate contractor management plan (CMP) appendix or in appropriate sections of operation plans (OPLANs) and operation orders (OPORDs). The CMP should specify government furnished support (life support, transportation support, FP, etc.) when such support is required. It should also provide guidance on other key contractor management procedures such as incorporating in-theater contractor movements, the use of contracted security, and coordinating other government agency (OGA) contract support actions.

(2) **Predeployment actions** include those actions taken by the government and the contract companies to ensure that CAAF are properly prepared to deploy in support of military operations. Predeployment actions include, but are not limited to, establishing appropriate contingency clause requirements in all appropriate contracts, establishing and promulgating specific theater entrance requirements and completing these theater entrance requirements prior to deployment.

(3) **Deployment and reception** involves managing the flow of CAAF into the designated joint operations area (JOA), including establishment of joint reception centers

(JRCs) and procedures for contractor personnel entering the JOA. The process ends once the contractor personnel arrive at the contract site of performance.

(4) **In-theater management** involves orchestrating and managing the provision of day-to-day support to CAAF, to include the enforcement of rules and regulations governing conduct of contractor personnel, processing of arming requests, and provision of government-provided support. This stage ends once CAAF redeploy out of the designated operational area.

(5) **Redeployment** involves orchestrating the redeployment of the CAAF out of the designated JOA, once their period of performance ends. This stage may include transportation back to the point of entry, life support enroute to the point of entry, intelligence debriefings, medical surveillance, and retrieval of military issued ID cards and personal equipment.

CHAPTER II
ROLES AND RESPONSIBILITIES

> *"A lot of what we have done in terms of reducing the size of active and reserve component force structure means there's a greater reliance on contractors. And there's a lot of technology that requires contractor support."*
>
> **David McKiernan, Lieutenant General,**
> **Third Army Commander, *Atlanta Constitution,* 2003**

1. Introduction

This chapter outlines the roles, relationships, and responsibilities of DOD, joint, and Service commanders and staffs related to operational contract support. Planning and managing contracted support and its associated contractor personnel integration actions involves numerous command and staff elements. Understanding the roles and responsibilities of these organizations is critically important to all commands and staffs that may be involved with planning and managing contracted support and contractor management.

2. Office of the Secretary of Defense

a. **Secretary of Defense** (SecDef) operational contract support responsibilities fall into two general areas: those related to defense acquisition and those related to the assignment and attachment of the forces to the combatant organizations necessary to carry out joint operations. Contracted support and associated contractor management actions involve all levels of commands. SecDef is responsible for **issuing directives, instructions, and executing oversight** on the force apportionment process. In some cases, the Office of the Secretary of Defense (OSD) may be called upon to assist the supported GCC in resolving and/or providing guidance related to specific organization C2, legal, funding, or other contracting or contractor management operational issues.

b. The **Under Secretary of Defense for Acquisition, Technology, and Logistics** (USD(AT&L)) serves as the Defense Acquisition Executive and has overall responsibility for the performance of the DOD Acquisition System, including establishing and publishing policies and procedures governing the operations of the DOD Acquisition System and the administrative oversight of defense contracts. While these responsibilities are more traditionally associated with oversight of systems acquisition, USD(AT&L) is also responsible to develop and oversee the implementation of DOD-level operational contract support policy. Assistants charged with carrying out related responsibilities include:

(1) The **Director, Defense Procurement and Acquisition Policy (DPAP)** oversees the development and administration of contracting policy and DFARS. Specific Director, DPAP responsibilities include:

(a) Developing DOD contracting policy and issuing necessary directives for effective contingency contracting support to joint operations during contingency and crisis planning and during actual contingency operations. DPAP operationally focused memoranda may include, but are not limited to, memoranda related to contracting authority, contract delegations, and coordinating relationships.

(b) Leading and coordinating efforts of Military Department senior procurement executives, including actions related to GCC support.

(c) Leading the Defense Emergency Procurement Committee (EPC). The EPC develops solutions to emergent procurement issues affecting the execution of contingency contracting in various contingencies.

(d) Leading the Defense Acquisition Regulation (DAR) Council and associated working groups. The DAR council maintains the DFARS, including contingency related clauses, procedures, guidance, and information (PGI) and other language necessary to tie the contracting process to contingency support. The DAR Council members also participate in development of FAR language as part of the FAR Council and associated working groups.

(e) Ensuring that DOD-level contingency contracting related issues requiring legislative relief are worked with Congress.

(2) **Deputy Under Secretary of Defense for Logistics and Material Readiness**, through the **Assistant Deputy Under Secretary of Defense (Program Support)**, is responsible for monitoring and managing the implementation contractor management policy. Specific responsibilities include:

(a) Develop, promulgate, and administer DOD contractor management policy in the accordance with DODI 3020.41, *Contractor Personnel Authorized to Accompany the US Armed Forces*. This regulation provides overarching guidance and serves as a comprehensive source of DOD-level policies and procedures concerning the integration of CAAF into military operations.

(b) In conjunction with Under Secretary of Defense for Personnel and Readiness (USD[P&R]), ensure that a joint web-based contract visibility and contractor accountability system is designated and implemented, along with procedures for its use.

(c) Assist the supported CCDR in addressing issues and actions related to contractor management requirements and supporting contracting activities across DOD.

c. **USD(P&R)** is the primary staff assistant and advisor to SecDef for total force management. USD(P&R) is responsible for policy, plans, and program development for the total force, which includes military, DOD civilian, and DOD contractor personnel. Responsibilities relevant to contractor personnel management include:

(1) In coordination with USD(AT&L), establish the central repository for CAAF accountability information.

(2) Develop, promulgate, and administer DOD ID policy and procedures to include specific guidance on ID issuance to CAAF personnel.

(3) Establish and issue guidance IAW DODI 1100.4, *Guidance for Manpower Management,* and DODD 1100.22, *Guidance for Determining Workforce Mix*, to be used by all DOD components regarding manpower management, including manpower mix criteria, to ensure that contracted services are not inherently governmental or inherently military or otherwise unsuitable or not allowed for commercial performance.

d. **The Under Secretary of Defense for Intelligence** is responsible for developing and implementing, as required, procedures for counterintelligence (CI) and security screenings of contingency contractor personnel and assisting in drafting appropriate contract clauses for CI briefings and debriefings, in coordination with (ICW) the USD(AT&L).

e. **The Assistant Secretary of Defense for Health Affairs** is responsible for developing and implementing, as required, policies and procedures for medical preparation, screening, and base-line health service support requirements of contractor personnel operating in support of contingency operations.

f. **The Deputy Assistant Secretary of Defense, Defense POW/Missing Personnel Office (DPMO)** is designated as the office of primary responsibility by the Assistant Secretary of Defense for Global Security Affairs for PR policy and oversight. As the DOD lead for PR, DPMO is responsible for the coordination among the Services, the Joint Staff (JS), the Unified and Combatant Commands, and with all other departments and agencies of the USG on all matters concerning the isolation of CAAF (and any non-CAAF specifically designated by the GCC or subordinate JFC) from friendly control. DPMO also has the following specific responsibilities:

(1) Account for those CAAF who remain missing when PR efforts have been deemed no longer feasible.

(2) Track circumstances of loss; monitor efforts to locate support, recover CAAF isolated from friendly control, and oversee the reintegration of CAAF.

(3) Oversee the implementation of the Missing Service Personnel Act (MSPA) to include investigation of circumstances surrounding the missing (currently and post-conflict), staff recommendations to the Under Secretary of Defense for Policy that missing CAAF are covered under the MSPA, and Service Chiefs of concern follow through with assignment of a binding status, and lead efforts that would ultimately result in the recovery and return of human remains.

g. **The Office of General Counsel** provides advice to the SecDef and Deputy Secretary of Defense regarding all legal matters and services performed within, or involving, the DOD and legal advice to OSD organizations and, as appropriate, other DOD components. Responsibilities pertinent to operational contract support include:

(1) Provide advice on legal matters, including law of war, military justice, and standards of conduct for civilians authorized to accompany the force.

(2) Provide legal review and positions related to FAR and DFARS language.

(3) Coordinate DOD positions on legislation and executive orders.

(4) Provide for the coordination of significant legal issues, including litigation involving the DOD and other matters before the Department of Justice in which DOD has an interest.

(5) Determine the DOD positions on specific legal problems and resolve disagreements within the DOD on such matters.

(6) Act as lead counsel for DOD in all international negotiations conducted by OSD organizations.

(7) Maintain the central repository for all international agreements (e.g., acquisition and cross-servicing agreements [ACSAs] and status-of-forces agreements [SOFAs]) coordinated or negotiated by DOD personnel.

3. Chairman of the Joint Chiefs of Staff

a. **The Chairman of the Joint Chiefs of Staff (CJCS)**, as the **principal military advisor** to the President and the SecDef, has specific responsibilities in the areas of strategic direction as well as in strategic and contingency planning. CJCS and principal staff responsibilities related to contracting support and contractor management is described below.

b. **The Joint Staff J-1** establishes the manpower management, personnel support, and personnel service support policies and procedures for the total force (military, DOD civilian, and DOD contractor) during joint operations and administers oversight of joint personnel issues affecting the force. This includes coordinating manpower and personnel support to combatant commanders to ensure success in operations. Key responsibilities are to:

(1) Assist the USD(P&R), USD(AT&L), and Joint Staff Logistics Directorate (J-4) in achieving resolution of personnel service support issues relating to CAAF in joint operations.

(2) Establish policy for the accountability of CAAF on the joint personnel status report.

(3) Provide total force strength data and casualty reporting of personnel in a GCC's area of responsibility (AOR) to CJCS for situational awareness.

(4) Provide input, if deemed appropriate by JS J-1, to Joint Staff Operational Plans and Joint Force Development Directorate (J-7), on the integration of personnel service support for CAAF in the CJCS Exercise Program.

(5) Coordinate military CAAF deployment actions in support of joint operations to include CAAF documented on a validated joint manning document (JMD).

c. **The Joint Staff J-2.** The primary role of the JS J-2 in contracting support is to communicate policy originating from the Under Secretary of Defense for Intelligence to the combatant commands. The JS J-2 establishes procedures through joint doctrine for combatant commands to ensure proper vetting, for intelligence, CI, and FP purposes, of locally employed persons contracted by US forces to support US and coalition efforts.

(1) In general, the JS J-2 is responsible for overseeing the activities of the combatant commands, to include the effectiveness of CI support, integrating that support into strategic and joint plans.

(2) The JS J-2 CI provides joint CI staff planning support to the CJCS. They review the CI component of combatant command war plans and contingency operations for the JS J-2. They perform requirements management duties at the DOD level for external CI requirements identified by the counterintelligence support office (CISO) during combatant command mission analysis of contingency plans.

For more information on CI responsibilities and activities, see Joint Publication (JP) 2-01.2, Counterintelligence and Human Intelligence Support to Joint Operations, *(classified).*

d. **The Joint Staff J-3** develops and provides guidance to the combatant commands regarding current operations and plans, including:

(1) Ensuring contracted support and associated contractor integration requirements are addressed in the JOPES policy and execution.

(2) Providing the CJCS with recommended rules for the use of force (RUF) by private security contractors and contractor personnel armed for personal protection, in support of joint operations.

e. **The Joint Staff J-4** provides plans, policy, guidance, and oversight on joint logistics, including joint contingency operational contract support matters. Specific responsibilities include:

(1) Develop and promulgate operational contract support planning policy.

(2) Facilitate communication of operational contract-related matters through routine meetings and communications with the joint community of interest.

(3) Participate in USD(AT&L), DPAP and Assistant Deputy Under Secretary of Defense (Program Support)-led working groups and other OSD-led actions affecting joint contingency contracting and contractor management.

(4) Participate in DAR Council working groups in the development of contract language and clauses in the FAR and DFARS.

(5) Participate in various joint and multinational joint contingency contracting and contractor management working groups and share lessons learned.

(6) In coordination with the CCDRs, the Military Departments, and the DOD combat support agencies, help facilitate OSD efforts to develop and implement CAAF accountability policy, procedures, and materiel solutions.

(7) Facilitate OSD efforts to implement contractor management related policy within the Military Departments, CCDRs, and DOD agencies.

(8) Facilitate efforts to incorporate joint contingency contracting and contractor management related content into joint professional military education (JPME) and CJCS exercises.

(9) Ensure operational contract support is incorporated into the CCDR OPLANs.

f. **The Joint Staff J-5**

(1) Ensure operational contract support policies and procedures are included in overarching policy documents to facilitate military operations.

(2) Ensure CAAF are included into the planning policies for deployment and redeployment (e.g., if applicable, included into the time-phased force and deployment data [TPFDD]).

g. **The Joint Staff J-6.** Joint Community Warfighter Chief Information Officer provides advice and recommendations on information technology and national security systems matters to the CJCS including technical support to the J-3 and J-4 for assessment of communications requirements in combatant command plans that require contracted support.

h. **The Joint Staff J-7** mission is to enhance joint force development and transformation initiatives through war plans, doctrine, education, training, exercises, concept development, capabilities-based planning, and assessment of each through observation of combatant command and CJCS experimentation, joint exercises, and real-world operations. Pertinent responsibilities include integration of contractor management related collective training requirements for Joint Chiefs of Staff exercises and JPME programs.

i. **The Joint Staff Legal Counsel** provides legal advice and guidance to the CJCS and other members of the Joint Staff and the combatant commands, as directed. Specific operational contract support responsibilities include:

(1) Reviewing and coordinating policy, plans, and other guidance.

(2) Participating in related working groups.

(3) Maintaining strategic awareness on evolving issues affecting joint contingency contracting and the integration of CAAF in joint operations.

(4) Providing legal review of the operational contract support aspects of joint force operations OPORDs, fragmentary orders (FRAGORDs), and OPLANs.

4. Military Departments

a. **The Secretaries of the Military Departments are responsible for the administration and support of the forces assigned or attached to combatant commands.** One way that they fulfill their responsibilities **is by augmenting military support capabilities with contracted support** through their respective Service component commands assigned to the combatant commands. The Military Departments exercise contracting authority and responsibilities codified under US laws, the FAR, DOD policy, CJCS policy, as well as joint and Service doctrine.

b. **The Army, Marine Corps, Navy, and Air Force (under their respective Secretaries) are responsible for planning and executing contracting support to their own forces unless directed otherwise by a CCDR as described in Chapter III, "Contract Support Integration."** Specific Military Department roles and responsibilities include:

(1) Ensure operational contract support requirements are identified and integrated into OPLANs.

(2) Ensure contractor management plans are incorporated into OPLANs.

(3) Ensure contracting requirements are captured and translated into draft statements of work with well defined performance parameters.

(4) Develop and publish contract support integration plans to synchronize contracted support. Analyze existing and projected theater and external support contracts to minimize redundant and overlapping contracts and maximize economies of effort and scale to improve operational unity of effort.

(5) Ensure contracted support to other services, DOD agencies, multinational partners, and OGA are addressed and priorities of effort for resources are de-conflicted and synchronized.

(6) Ensure contracted support movement (regardless if provided by the government or the contractor) in support of an operation is incorporated into OPLAN TPFDD.

(7) Develop contingency plans to ensure continuation of essential contractor services.

(8) Enforce established theater and/or JOA CAAF admission procedures and requirements, including country and theater clearance, waiver authority, immunizations, required training or equipment, and any restrictions necessary to ensure proper deployment, visibility, security, accountability, and redeployment of CAAF personnel deploying to their AOR.

(9) Integrate identified contract requirements into training simulations, mission rehearsals, and exercises.

(10) Ensure military personnel outside the acquisition workforce who are expected to have acquisition responsibility, including oversight duties associated with contracts or contractors, during combat operations, post-conflict operations, and contingency operations are properly trained.

(11) Ensure contract oversight management processes and manpower requirements to execute oversight are adequately incorporated into OPLANs.

(12) Collect and distribute operational contract support lessons learned.

(13) Determine the COR requirements and required qualifications and ensure that CORs are properly trained and certified.

(14) When required, delegate HCA authority as directed by one of the established contracting activities within the various military services.

5. Combatant Commanders and Subordinate Joint Force Commanders

a. **Supported CCDRs** play a key role in determining and synchronizing contracted support requirements, contracting planning as well as execution of operational contract support oversight. The supported CCDR must work very closely with the appropriate subordinate JFCs, functional combatant commands, Service components, and DOD combat support agencies to determine operational contract support requirements, policies, and procedures. Supported CCDRs' specific contracting support and contractor management roles and responsibilities include, but are not limited to:

(1) Developing and publishing applicable regulations, instructions, and directives for the conduct of efficient and effective synchronization of operational contract support.

(2) Developing a CSIP as part of every OPLAN or OPORD that includes specific contract support integration related organizational guidance and lead Service or joint theater support contracting command responsibilities as applicable.

(3) Establishing, manning, and executing appropriate operational contract support related boards, centers, and working groups.

(4) Developing and promulgating contractor management plans to include theater entrance requirements for all CAAF to include specific delineation of the differences between US citizens and non-US citizens in government furnished support standards.

(5) Integrating and controlling the deployment of CAAF and contractor equipment.

(6) Planning and managing CAAF government furnished support requirements.

(7) In coordination with the Joint Staff, reviewing, developing, and promulgating predeployment training standards for CAAF.

b. **The subordinate JFC, a subunified command, or joint task force commander** play a key role in determining specific contracted support requirements, contracting planning, as well as execution of operational contract support oversight within a specified operational area. Working very closely with the Service components and other elements of the joint force, the subordinate JFC's specific contract support roles and responsibilities include, but are not limited to:

(1) Determining contracted support and integration requirements across the joint force to include DOD agencies, multinational partners, and OGAs.

(2) Determining and promulgating CCDR approved operational contract support related organizational guidance in the appropriate OPLAN, OPORD, or FRAGORD.

(3) Developing and promulgating CSIPs as required with focus on maximizing effectiveness of support via unity of effort.

(4) Establishing and enforcing priorities of contract support across the joint force, multinational partners, and OGAs.

(5) Developing and promulgating specific operational CAAF related requirements if not already covered by GCC policy, directives, and orders.

(6) Developing and enforcing operational specific contractor management requirements, directives, and procedures into a separate contractor management appendix to annex W and/or the appropriate section of the appropriate OPLAN, OPORD or FRAGORD.

(7) Ensuring contractor personnel receive necessary government furnished support as required by operational conditions and that this support is properly coordinated between the component commands.

c. **The functional combatant commanders and their staffs** play a limited role in planning and managing operational contract support in support of military operations.

(1) **USSOCOM** forces have their own theater support contracting authority and capabilities, but will still often request CUL related contracting support from the lead Service or joint theater support contracting organization. In all operations, USSOCOM and supported JFC contracting efforts must be closely coordinated.

(2) **US TRANSCOM** also has its own contracting authority. USTRANSCOM contracted support generally involves strategic transportation contracts which have an area of performance outside the operational area; however, in some cases this support may be partially executed in the operational area. In these situations, USTRANSCOM is responsible to coordinate with the supported GCC as required. Additionally, USTRANSCOM's surface component command, the Surface Deployment and Distribution Command (SDDC), may be designated as the port manager and/or operator within an operational area. When so designated, SDDC will depend on the Army Service component command or lead Service component responsible for contracting support to assist them in procuring stevedore support via theater support contracts in support of port operations.

(3) **US Joint Forces Command** is responsible for examining evolving operational contract support issues in the appropriate concept, experimentation, and doctrine development actions. They are also responsible to ensure that key joint operational contract support challenges are incorporated into joint training venues as deemed appropriate.

6. Service Component Commands

The Army, Marine Corps, Navy, and Air Force Service component commands are responsible for planning and executing contracting support IAW the guidance received from their respective Military Departments and supported JFC. Specific operational contract support related Service component roles and responsibilities include, but are not limited to:

a. Unless otherwise directed, providing HCA over Service theater support contracting organizations within their operational area.

b. Executing or supporting lead Service contracting responsibilities as directed.

c. Analyzing existing and projected Service theater support and DOD-wide external support contracts in order to reduce any redundancy and maximize economy of effort.

d. Enforcing JFC established priorities of contract support across the joint force, multinational partners, and OGAs.

e. Determining operational specific contracting and contract management personnel force requirements and capturing these requirements in Service component CSIPs, per JFC guidance.

f. Ensuring funds are available to support contract requirements.

g. Developing and enforcing policies and directives that are based on JFC and military Service guidance.

h. Ensuring all CAAF meet specific theater entrance requirements prior to deployment to the operational area.

i. Ensuring all CAAF and their associated equipment are properly incorporated into deployment plans regardless if this deployment is via military means or self-supported.

j. Ensuring subordinate units are prepared to execute operational contract support responsibilities to include developing "acquisition ready" requirements packages consisting of PWSs, IGEs, and other contract related documents as necessary and by providing trained CORs as required.

k. Executing operational specific collective and individual contract support integration and contract management training requirements.

l. Developing contingency plans to ensure continuation of essential contractor services, per DOD policy.

m. Collecting and distributing operational contract support lessons learned to the appropriate Service lessons learned program.

7. Functional Component Commands

In general, the air, land, and maritime functional component commands (if established) are not directly responsible for operational contract support actions. Contracting support is a Service Title 10 USC, responsibility that normally falls under the auspices of the Service component commands and this authority is not normally transferred to joint air, land, or maritime functional commands.

See JP 1, Doctrine for the Armed Forces of the United States, *Chapter V,* "Doctrine for Joint Commands", *for more information on joint functional component commands.*

8. Department of Defense Agencies

a. **The Defense Logistics Agency** is the DOD combat support agency responsible for providing effective and efficient worldwide logistics support to Military Departments and the combatant commands under conditions of peace and war, as well as to other DOD components and federal agencies, and when authorized by law, state and local government organizations, foreign governments and intergovernmental organizations (IGOs). The DLA Director reports to the USD(AT&L) through the Deputy Under Secretary of Defense for Logistics and Materiel Readiness. DLA also has its own contracting authority and can provide supply and service contracting during contingency operations.

Appendix D, "Defense Logistics Agency Contingency Contracting Functions and Capabilities"*, provides more details on the capabilities and deployed organizational structure of DLA.*

b. The **Defense Contract Management Agency (DCMA)** is the combat support agency responsible for ensuring major DOD acquisition programs (systems, supplies, and services) are delivered on time, within projected cost or price, and meet performance requirements. DCMA's major role and responsibilities in contingency operations is to provide CCAS for delegated external support contracts and for selected weapons systems support contracts with place of performance in the operational area and theater support contracts when CCAS is delegated by the PCO.

Appendix D, "Defense Contract Management Agency Contingency Functions and Capabilities" *provides more details on the capabilities and deployed organizational structure of DCMA.*

c. The **Defense Contract Audit Agency (DCAA)** is a defense agency under the authority, direction, and control of the Under Secretary of Defense (Comptroller). DCAA is responsible for performing all contract audits for the DOD, and providing accounting and financial advisory services regarding contracts and subcontracts to all DOD components responsible for procurement and contract administration. These services are provided in connection with negotiation, administration, and settlement of contracts and subcontracts. DCAA also provides contract audit services to OGAs on a reimbursable basis. DCAA's services are provided under contingency contracting situations, both in support of military operations and during a national emergency. DCAA personnel can be deployed, as circumstances warrant, to the operational area. DCAA on site auditors are responsible to identify practices needing improvement on a real-time basis and recommend cost avoidance opportunities to selected contingency contracts.

CHAPTER III
CONTRACT SUPPORT INTEGRATION

> *"The role of federal contractors has been expanding in the areas of front-line and near front-line support for the United States military and other government agencies. Both the war with Iraq and the ongoing war on terrorism have increased the demand for the services of contractors in so-called "hot zones,..."*
>
> **Various Sources**

1. Overview

This chapter provides an overview of contract support integration planning and execution across the range of military operations. It provides the GCC, subordinate JFC, Military Department components, and other members of the joint force important information on contracting authorities, acquisition processes, types of contracted support, and contracting support planning, along with significant discussion on in-theater contracting organizational structure. It also provides guidance on special contract support related challenges to include multinational, interagency, reconstruction, and homeland security operations.

a. Contracting for supplies and services in support of military operations is a force multiplier. Contracting is commonly used to augment organic military and other sources of support such as multinational logistic support, HNS, and to provide support where no organic capability exists, but contracting is often not properly planned for or integrated into the overall joint force logistic support effort. Contracting support capabilities should be considered when needed to augment organic support capabilities and in situations where ACSAs or HNS agreements do not exist or when these agreements cannot provide sufficient supplies or services.

b. **Determining the appropriate source of CUL support and priorities of this support is not a contracting function.** The supported GCC must ensure that there is a joint acquisition review board (JARB) or JARB-like process in place at the appropriate level (normally at the subunified command or joint task force (JTF) level) to determine the basic source of support and priority of CUL requirements. The joint force must be aware of the considerable challenges that exist to successfully execute a contract when contracted support is determined to be the only source of acquisition. When the decision is made to pursue contracted support, there are considerable challenges associated with planning and execution. These challenges include, but are not limited to: developing a complete requirements package, coordinating the overall contracting effort, executing the effort IAW federal law and regulation, and ensuring adequate in-theater contract oversight and management.

See paragraph 3 along with Appendix G, "Requirements Development and Acquisition Review Processes", *for more information on the overall acquisition process.*

(1) **Centralized Control and Decentralized Execution.** Contracting operates under two premises: centralized control (or at least coordination) and decentralized

execution. Centralized control can either be accomplished by mandating local procurement procedures through subordinate JFC contracting boards and/or through the designation of a lead Service or joint theater support contracting command. The decentralized execution premise is accomplished through the procurement authority vested in the contracting officer to exercise business judgment in the execution of the contracting mission. The FAR, DFARS, and local procurement policies may also mandate reviews of certain contractual actions prior to the contracting officer signature.

(2) **Coordination.** The supported GCC and subordinate JFC are responsible for properly synchronizing and coordinating all of the different contracting support actions being planned for and executed in the operational area. It is very important that contracting efforts are properly coordinated with all subordinate commands and DOD agencies, as well as applicable multinational, OGAs, IGOs, and nongovernmental organizations (NGOs). This coordination is necessary in order to prevent undue competition for the same limited commercial resources in the operational area. Coordination also provides the JFC the ability to enforce priorities and control common logistic support efforts and maximize the use and/or utility of the limited contracting force.

(3) **Federal Law and Regulation.** The GCC, subordinate JFCs, and their staffs must be cognizant of the fact that contracted support for any military operation is planned for and executed IAW federal law and the FAR. **Although the contracting officers have wide latitude to exercise business judgment to accomplish their mission, they do not have authority to deviate from statutory requirements.**

(4) **In-theater Contract Management.** The GCC, subordinate JFCs, and supporting commanders must understand that **contracting is not a "fire and forget" process.** Contracting support to military operations requires significant planning and management efforts from the contracting staff, the requiring activity, and supporting activities. The JFC and component commanders must ensure that the requiring activities are properly trained and actively participate in the requirements generation and validation process. Requiring activities typically provide personnel to serve as contracting officer appointed representatives. These personnel require formal, requisite training in order to serve as ordering officials, FOOs, government purchase card (GPC) holders, or CORs. Ordering officials will be trained and certified to make individual orders from blanket purchase agreements. FOOs are individuals authorized to make micro-purchases for construction, supplies, and services using the SF-44. The actual dollar limits for these items may change, but is generally limited to micro-purchase threshold amounts specified in the FAR. For service-type contracts, the JFC and component commanders must ensure that all supported units have sufficient number of certified COR personnel available to monitor contractor performance. Additional non-COR support, such as personnel to perform security checks and/or escort the contractors, may also be required. For cost plus contracts, there is also a periodic need to revalidate requirements and ensure that the contractor is operating efficiently. Without proper command involvement and contract management capabilities in place, the JFC is likely to experience significantly increased operational costs, and more importantly, possible loss of operational effectiveness and increased security risks.

CONTRACTING IN OPERATION IRAQI FREEDOM

During 2004-2005 rotation to Operation IRAQI FREEDOM, the 1st Aviation Brigade, 4th Infantry Division had a requirement to renovate a building on forward operating base (FOB) Taji. In order to get this project approved by the joint acquisition review board (JARB) and joint facilities utilization board (JFUB), they were required by established joint force commander policy to develop a performance work statement (PWS) and independent government estimate (IGE). Since they had no engineering expertise on staff, they requested assistance from the designated FOB engineering office, the Air Force Red Horse Engineering Detachment, to assist in developing these documents. Once this was accomplished, the unit submitted the IGE, an approved DA 3953 purchase request and commitment form, and a letter of justification to the JARB and JFUB. Once approved, the packet was sent to Joint Contracting Command-Iraq/Afghanistan, which assigned it to the regional contracting center (RCC) located at FOB Taji. A contracting officer within RCC Taji was assigned and then prepared the solicitation, compared bids, awarded the contract to a local vendor, and issued a notice to proceed. Once the contract was awarded, the local vendor had 30 days to complete all work not including Friday "Holy Days" and any delays caused by the government. Since this was a service contract, RCC Taji required the unit to provide a contracting officer representative to ensure work was completed in accordance with the PWS. Additionally, since the vendor and his employees were local nationals, the unit was required to provide an armed escort for these employees for the entire period of performance. In accordance with FOB Taji security policy, this particular contract required one armed unit guard for every ten local national personnel. This particular contract had between 12 and 18 employees working on the building each day. The armed escort had to meet the vendor at the FOB gate to process them onto the base, escort them to the work site, guard them through the workday and then escort them off the FOB not later than 1700hrs each day. Once the work was complete and accepted by the RCC, the unit was responsible to escort the vendor to finance to receive his payment. The renovation took approximately 70 days to complete from the time of identification of the requirement to time of completion of the work.

SOURCE: Contracting Officer, Taji Regional Contracting Center

2. Contracting Authority Versus Command Authority

Contracting authority is not the same as command authority. Contracting authority is the legal authority to enter into binding contracts and obligate funds for the USG, while command includes the authority and responsibility for effectively using available resources and for planning the employment of, organizing, directing, coordinating, and controlling military forces for the accomplishment of assigned missions. Command authority does not include the authority to obligate funds or enter into contracts on behalf of the government.

Hence, these two different authorities must be closely coordinated to ensure effective and efficient contracted support to the joint force.

a. **Contracting Authority.** A unique aspect of contracting support is that only the contracting officer has the authority to obligate the USG. This authority to acquire supplies and services for the government comes from three sources: the US Constitution; statutory authority; and finally, regulatory authority from the FAR, DFARS, and Military Department supplements. Contracting authority in the operational area flows from Congress to the President, then to the SecDef, through the Service/agency head, to the HCA, then to the SCO, and finally to the contracting officer. This contracting authority is explicitly documented via the contracting officer's warrant. A warrant is the document that authorizes a contracting officer to obligate the government to expend funds for contracted support requirements. Any restrictions on a contracting officer's authority to purchase items will be explicitly stated on the warrant. The most common restriction is placed on the maximum amount a contracting officer is authorized to obligate per contract award. Another common restriction limits the types of contracts a contracting officer is authorized to award. Contingency contracting authority resides in all Military Departments, USSOCOM, and the DOD combat support agencies, such as DLA. For classified requirements, the contracting officer and CORs may be required to have a security clearance.

b. **Command Authority.** Combatant command (command authority), prescribed in Title 10 USC, Section 164, includes the authority to perform functions involving organizing and employing commands and forces, assigning tasks and designating objectives, and giving authoritative direction over all aspects of an operation; it **does not include authority to make binding contracts for the USG.** Only the contracting officer, by virtue of their contracting warrant, has the contracting authority to obligate the USG on contractual matters. Contingency contracting authority flows to the contracting officer through the Service, DLA, DCMA, and USSOCOM HCAs. **It is also important to note that GCCs do not have their own contracting authority.** The GCCs direct and coordinate contingency contracting support through their subordinate Service components, USSOCOM, and deployed combat support agency organizations.

c. **Command and Control of Contracting Organizations.** Due to the unique nature of contracting authority, established C2 relationships, as defined in JP 1, *Doctrine for the Armed Forces of the United States,* are not easily applied to contracting units. In general, joint or lead Service C2 over contracting forces outside normal Service C2 lines only applies to theater support contracting organizations. C2 of theater support contracting organizations is discussed in detail in Paragraph 6.

d. **Avoiding Undue Command Influence.** Commanders at all levels must take care to avoid improper command influence, or its appearance, on the contracting process. The contracting officer must be able to independently exercise sound, unbiased business judgment and contract oversight in the accomplishment of the contracting mission. Contracting officers can only fulfill their responsibilities for safeguarding the interests of the USG in its contractual relationships through functional independence from the requiring activity, allowing them to properly execute their business judgment in the formation, negotiation, award, and administration of contracts. Subordinate JFCs and Service component commanders must ensure that requirements personnel only have influence on the requirements definition and in no way influence the contracting officer's contract award decision. If there is a valid, certified operational need to direct contracts to specific commercial sources, such as in stability operations where the JFC needs to balance civil-military impacts and cost-effectiveness of specific contracts, the contingency HCA is responsible for developing policies to implement this aspect of the OPLAN with appropriate contracting procedures IAW federal law and the FAR.

IMPROPER COMMAND INFLUENCE

During 2006 Operation IRAQI FREEDOM, a regional contracting office (RCO) was busy processing multiple contracting requests from numerous units in northern Iraq. Due to the limited staffing within the RCO, procedures were established to ensure that unit contracting requests were prioritized and processed in accordance with established joint force commander guidance. It was not uncommon for the regional contracting center (RCC) staff to have discussions with supported unit personnel on how they handled competing requests and why they could not deviate from established contracting priorities and procedures. In this case, a mid-level commander approached one of his assigned contracting officers working in the RCO with a funded purchase request for general labor and stated that he wanted a sole source contract with one of the local vendors. After the contracting officer told the commander that there was no valid justification for a sole source contract, the commander threatened that this finding could negatively affect the contracting officer's future job performance rating. Immediately, the contracting officer notified the chief of RCC of the situation. Further discussion followed between the RCC chief and the commander on the legal aspects and operational reasons why contracting officers must be shielded from improper command influence on business decisions. Later, it was discovered the commander made an unauthorized commitment with the vendor to go sole source. Soon afterwards, a contract ratification was initiated against this commander for an amount of $6,000.

SOURCE: Interview with RCC chief

3. The Acquisition Process and Contracting Related Boards

a. It is very important that all CUL support be properly coordinated by the supported GCC and subordinate JFC to include contracting; however, determining the appropriate source of CUL support and establishing priorities of this support is not a contracting function. **The supported GCCs have directive authority for logistics, which includes the authority to issue directives to subordinate commanders, including peacetime measures necessary to ensure the following: effective execution of approved OPLANs;**

effectiveness and economy of operation; and prevention or elimination of unnecessary duplication of facilities and overlapping of functions among the Service component commands. In order to provide the subordinate JFC the ability to enforce priorities and control CUL support efforts, the supported GCC should strongly consider directing the establishment of three critically important contracting related review boards: the combatant commander logistic procurement support board (CLPSB), the JARB, and the joint contracting support board (JCSB). The establishment and membership of these boards will be dependent on the size and duration of the operation as well as other operational factors. In some instances, these boards may be combined. See Figure III-1.

b. The **CLPSB is established to ensure that contracting and other related logistics efforts are properly coordinated across the entire AOR.** This board is normally chaired by a GCC J-4 representative and includes representatives from each Service component command, combat support agency, as well as other military and USG agencies or organizations concerned with contracting matters.

c. **The JARB is a joint acquisition review board, not a contracting board.** The JARB is utilized to coordinate and control the requirements generation and prioritization of joint CUL supplies and services that are needed in support of the operational mission and is normally chaired by the subordinate JFC (either subunified command or JTF-level) or deputy commander or J-4. **The JARB's main role is to make specific approval and prioritization recommendations for all GCC directed, subordinate JFC controlled, high-value and/or high-visibility CUL requirements and to include recommendations on the proper source of support for these requirements.** The normal priority of CUL source of support include: lead Service organic military sources, multinational support, HNS, multinational military support, theater support contracts along with external support contracts such as the Military Department CAPs and DLA prime vendor contracts. The JARB is normally made up of representatives of the Service component logistic staffs, special operations forces (SOF) component staff, DLA, DCMA, joint force engineer, J-6, joint force comptroller, staff judge advocate (SJA), and other JFC staff members as directed. It also should include representatives from designated theater support and external support contracting organizations. The theater support and external support contracting members' main role in the JARB process is to inform the other JARB members which contracting mechanisms are readily available for their particular acquisition to include limits of the local vendor base for each type of support. This would facilitate the decision to use either external support contracts or theater support contracting assets.

d. **The JCSB is established in order to coordinate and deconflict contracting actions within the JOA.** The JCSB reviews contract support requirement forwarded by the JARB and makes recommendations on which specific contracting organizations/contract venues are best suited to fulfill the requirements. The JCSB is normally chaired by the subordinate J-4 acquisition officer or SCO. It is made up of representatives from the Service theater and external support contracting organizations (to include facility/engineering contracting), DCMA along with DLA, and SOF component contracting representatives. This process requires adequate visibility of CUL related contracting capabilities within the operational area, which can be a significant challenge. It is through this JCSB that the J-4

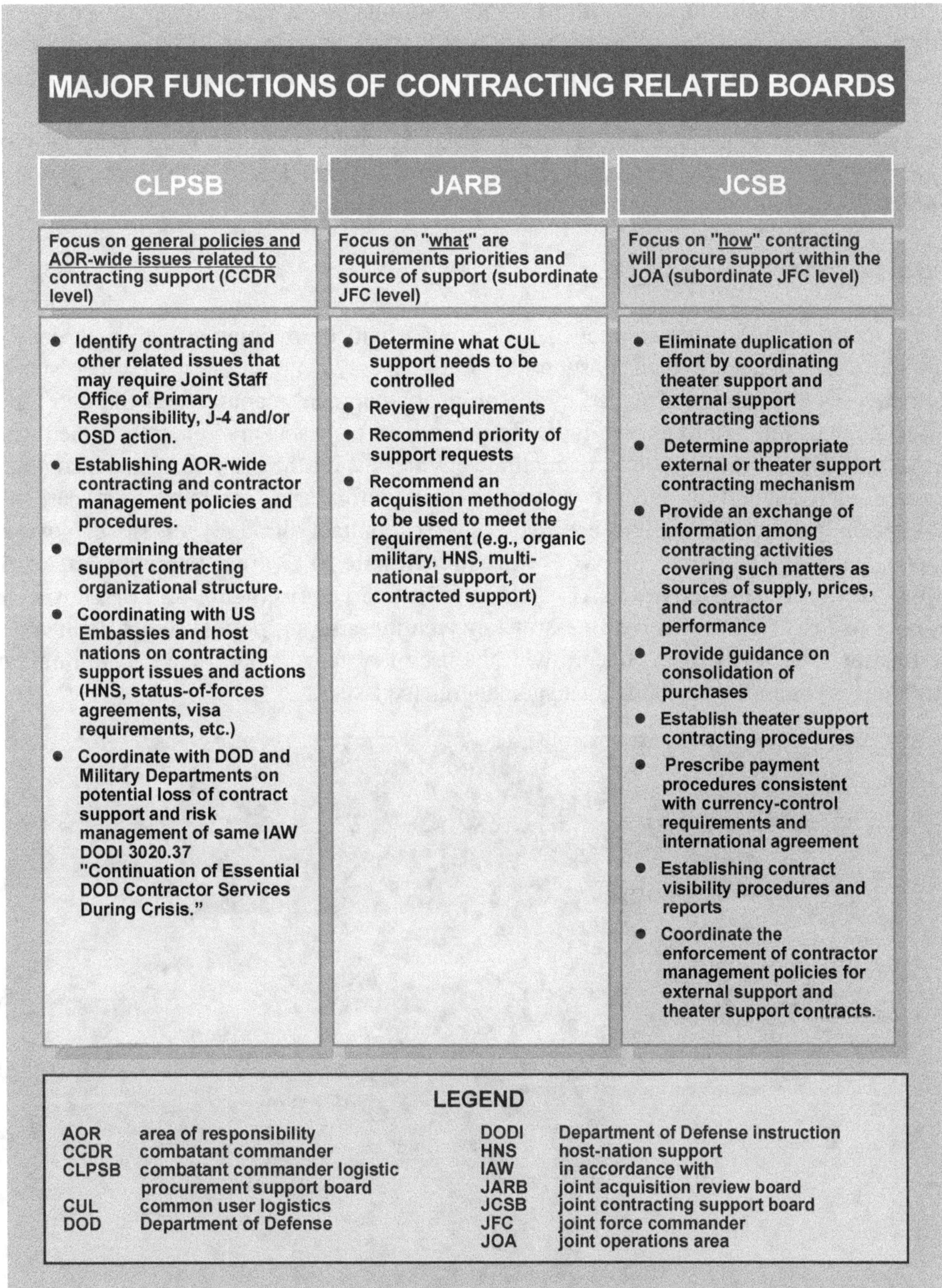

Figure III-1. Major Functions of Contracting Related Boards

ensures a coordinated contracting support effort across the entire operational area. **The goal of the JCSB is to maximize the contracting capabilities of the JOA while minimizing the competition for limited vendor capabilities.** It also establishes specific theater and external support contracting procedures and reporting requirements. While the CLPSB and

JCSB perform similar functions; the CLPSB coordinates general acquisition policy and addresses major contracting related issues across the AOR, while the JCSB is more focused on coordinating day-to-day contracting support within a specific JOA.

See Appendix G, "Requirements Development and Acquisition Review Processes," *for more details on the acquisition process. Also see JP 4-0,* Joint Logistics Support, *for more detailed discussion on joint logistic related boards and centers.*

4. Systems Support Contracting

a. Much of a Service component's equipment will be maintained either partially or fully through contracted logistic support. Often there is no military or other support alternative for the support provided by the original equipment manufacturer through FSRs, also sometimes referred to as tech-reps. These support contracts are generally issued when the Military Department systems contracting activities award the original systems contracts. Because such support is generally awarded long before and unrelated to a particular deployment requirement and is codified into the contract through generic deployment support language or clauses, the **GCC and subordinate JFC must be cognizant of the impact of overly restrictive CAAF theater entrance requirements and/or contracted support use restrictions on readiness of key weapon and support systems deployed to the theater.** The JFC's main concern with the use of systems support contracts in military operations is contractor personnel management related issues.

Three RQ-1 Predator field service representatives working at Balad Air Base, Iraq.

b. Individual Services need to ensure their systems support contracts contain appropriate deployment clauses IAW the FAR, DFARS, and adhere to DOD/Service policies. Prior to deploying contractor personnel into the operational area, systems support contracting officers, ICW the supported units, must ensure that contractor personnel have met specific theater entrance requirements. Additionally, the supported GCC and subordinate JFC must ensure that the theater entrance requirements and other operational specific contractor management directives are published, updated, and readily available to ensure systems support contractor personnel, the contracting officer, and supported units are aware of these requirements. This logistic support requirement and accountability of contractor personnel in the operational area are the main focus of the supported GCC and subordinate JFC in regard to planning and execution of systems support contracts.

DODI 3020.41, Contractor Personnel Authorized to Accompany the US Armed Forces, *is the primary DOD policy document that covers contractor personnel deployment and other contractor personnel integration policy. Integration of systems contractor personnel into military operations is also discussed in detail in Chapter IV,* "Contractor Management." *Additionally, an overview of the Service systems support contracts and management capabilities can be found in Appendix A,* "Services' Systems Support Contract Overview."

5. External Support Contracting

a. External support contracts are often used to provide significant logistic support and selected non-logistic support to the joint force as depicted in Figure III-2. The type and scope of this support varies between operations, but can be very extensive depending on a variety of operational factors. The three major logistic-related external support contract programs are the Army's LOGCAP, the Air Force's AFCAP and the Navy's GCCC/GCSC.

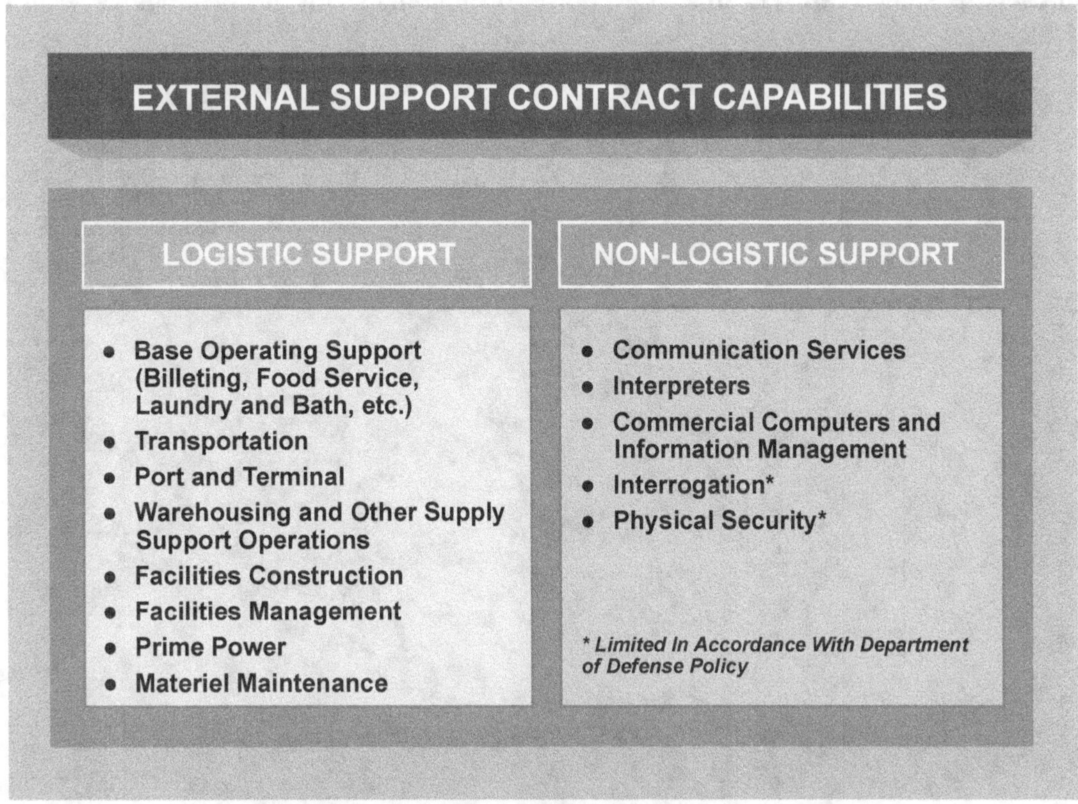

Figure III-2. External Support Contract Capabilities

Additionally, in some operations DLA may utilize existing or award new prime vendor contracts to provide selected supply support, primarily subsistence and bulk fuel, during contingency operations. Other examples of external support contracts include fuel contracts awarded by Defense Energy Support Center (DESC), construction contracts awarded by US Army Corps of Engineers and the Air Force Center for Engineering and the Environment, and translator contractors awarded by Army Intelligence and Security Command.

b. Like systems support contracts, **external support contracting authority does not come as a direct result of the contingency operation. Generally, these contracts are issued during peacetime for use during contingencies.** The Army's LOGCAP requirements are managed by the Army Sustainment Command (ASC) and the contracts are awarded and managed by the Army Contracting Command (ACC). ASC and ACC are major subordinate commands of the US Army Materiel Command (USAMC). What this means to the GCC is that contracting authority, and therefore the ability to modify the LOGCAP task orders, resides with USAMC (or designated DCMA ACOs), not with the theater support contracting HCA(s). **It is important to understand that these CAP and other external support contracts remain under the control of the Service components and do not normally fall under the authority of the GCC operational contract support.**

c. The JFC should be aware that **CAP support contracts are generally more expensive than theater support contracts** due to overhead, management, general, and administrative charges associated with external support contracts. Although logistic planners must make allowances for CAP contracts early in the contingency, **every effort should be made to transition the individual CAP task orders to theater support contracts as soon as practicable**. Of course, operation specific factors such as security

Logistic Civil Augmentation Program Team.

considerations, availability of local sources of support, and on-hand theater support contracting management capabilities will be the actual drivers of how many of, and how fast, these CAP task orders can be transferred to theater support contracts.

See Appendix B, "Services' External Support Contract Overview," *for more details on the Service CAP organizations and capabilities.*

6. Theater Support Contracting

a. **General Overview.** Theater support contracts are those contracts that are issued by deployed contingency contracting officers and are generally awarded to local vendors, to support in-theater customers. These contracts are specifically issued under the authority of the Service component and/or USSOCOM HCA designation for the contingency. Theater support contracts are those contracts that are most commonly referred to as contingency contracts. Theater support contracting can be used to acquire support from commercial sources similar to those external support contract services listed in Figure III-2. Additionally, theater support contracting can be used to acquire limited amounts of commercially available supply items from both local and global sources.

Contractor Open House in Afghanistan

b. **Establishing Joint or Lead Service Command and Control of Theater Support Contracting Organizations.** The supported GCC must designate the C2 authority that the joint or lead Service command will have over other Service theater support contracting organizations in complex, long-term operations to ensure effective and efficient theater contracting support to the joint force and/or designated OGAs. **However, because of the peculiar legal nature of contracting support, the lead Service or joint theater support contracting command must also have HCA authority over attached Service contingency contracting personnel. Since the supported GCC does not have the**

authority to direct changes to Service HCA authorities, establishing operational control (OPCON) relationships over theater support contracting units may require special coordination with the affected Military Departments and USD(AT&L). This combination of OPCON and HCA authority allows the lead Service or joint theater support contracting commander to set and enforce priorities; position and reposition contingency contracting personnel rapidly to the point of need; and to enforce contracting policies and compliance measures.

See Appendix C, "Services' Theater Support Contracting Organizations and Capabilities," *for more details on the Service theater support contracting organizations and capabilities.*

7. Contracting Support Organizational Options

a. **General.** There is no single preferred contracting organizational option; the specific organizational option is determined by the GCC ICW the subordinate JFC and Service components. **It is also important to note that these organizational options described below pertain to only theater support contacting individuals and organizations.** A designated lead Service or joint theater support contracting command would normally only have coordinating authority over Service component external support contracting organizations and DCMA's ACOs. These organizations, in general, have no authority over systems support contracts.

(1) There are **three main contracting related organizational options: Service component support to own forces; lead Service; and joint theater support contracting command.** These organizational options normally apply to the subordinate JFC-level. If there is no lead Service or joint theater support contracting command established, the subordinate JFC may establish a small contracting office as part of the subunified command or JTF J-4 staff. **This office would not have contracting authority; its main mission would be to assist the subordinate JFC in planning and coordinating operational contract support within the JOA.**

(2) The organizational option chosen is entirely dependent on the mission requirements and operational factors. These factors may include, but are not limited to:

(a) Size, primary mission, and expected duration of the joint operation.

(b) Scope, criticality, and complexity of the theater support contracting requirements.

(c) Need for enhanced JFC control of the theater support contracting mission.

(d) Location of supported units when compared to available commercial vendor base.

(e) Dominant user and most capable Service considerations (may not be the same Service in any given operation).

(3) Just as there is no one preferred option, the needs of the contracting organization may change as the operation progresses. Therefore, the contracting organizational structure may change and/or progress through the basic organizational options as the organizational needs unfold. Although the organizational structure may change over time, all organizational options must account for proper coordination and control of the overall theater support contracting actions in order to limit duplication of effort and service competition for limited vendor resources. The key point to consider in the choice of any contracting organizational option is that the organizational structure should be planned for in writing and should be a conscious choice prior to the onset of a contingency operation.

b. **Service Component Support to Own Forces.** During smaller scale operations with an expected short duration, the GCC would normally allow the Service component commanders to retain control of their own theater support contracting authority and organizations. This organizational option is also applicable to operations where the bulk of the individual Service component units will be operating in distinctly different areas of the JOA thus limiting potential competition for the same vendor base.

(1) **Advantages of Service Component Support to Own Forces:**

(a) Simplifies contracting procedures and processes.

(b) Does not require JMD.

(c) Does not require implementing new C2 relationships.

(d) Enhances trust of supported unit by retaining habitual relationships.

(2) **Disadvantages of Service Component Support to Own Forces:**

(a) May increase the likelihood of competition for limited local vendor base.

(b) May limit the JFC's ability to set and enforce priorities and standards of support.

(c) May limit the JFC's ability to standardize the acquisition process.

(d) May not be the most efficient use of the limited contracting staff.

c. **Lead Service Component Responsible for Theater Support Contracting**. The GCC may designate a specific Service component (normally the lead Service responsible for general CUL support) as the lead Service responsible to provide consolidated theater contracting support for a particular geographical region (normally the JOA). In most major operations, the lead Service will either be the Army or Air Force component due to the limited theater support contracting capabilities of the other Services.

(1) The lead Service organizational option is most appropriate for major, long-term operations where the supported GCC and subordinate JFC desire to ensure that there is a consolidated contracting effort within the operational area, but without the need to stand-up an entirely new joint command. In this option, the lead Service contracting organization may have C2 of designated other Service component theater support contracting organizations at a specified level and would have their staff augmented by other Services' contingency contracting personnel if approved by SecDef. Additionally a lead Service contracting organization could have coordination authority only as directed by the JFC (does not require SecDef approval). They also may have liaison officers from Service CAP management organizations, DLA, multinational military units, and/or IGOs, as required by the supported GCC. The lead Service SCO would normally chair the JCSB.

(2) **Advantages of Lead Service Option:**

(a) Decreases the likelihood of competition for limited local vendor base.

(b) Permits more efficient use of the limited contracting professional staff.

(c) Increases the JFC's ability to set and enforce priorities and establish a baseline for minimal standards for support.

(d) Increases the JFC's ability to standardize the acquisition process.

(3) **Disadvantages of Lead Service Option:**

(a) Will require implementing new C2 relationships.

(b) May initially decrease trust of the supported units.

(c) May require the development of a JMD.

(d) Requires specific command guidance to direct control over the theater support contracting effort.

d. **Joint Theater Support Contracting Command.** In larger or more complex contingency operations, the supported GCC may require more oversight than what can typically be provided through the lead Service organizational option.

(1) Operational conditions that may drive this option could include, but may not be limited to:

(a) Extremely complex operation that requires direct control of theater support contracting by the JFC.

(b) Mission is long-term duration.

(c) Mission beyond the capability of a single Service.

(d) Mission that requires significant coordination of contracting and the civil-military aspects of the OPLAN.

(e) Significant numbers of different Service forces operating in same area/joint bases served by the same local vendor base.

(f) The joint theater support contracting command, by design, is a joint functional command that has a specified level of C2 authority over designated Service component theater support contracting organizations and personnel within a designated support area. This command would perform the same functions as a lead Service contracting organization, but would report directly to the establishing commander.

(g) Since **GCCs do not have their own contracting authority, the joint theater support contracting command's HCA authority would flow from one of the Service components (normally the lead agent or lead Service component responsible for CUL) to the operational area.** In this option, the joint theater support contracting command headquarters (HQ) should be established by a JMD.

(2) If the GCC decides to establish a joint theater support contracting command, special consideration needs to be given to the placement of the legal support staff to avoid undue command influence of the new contracting command.

(3) **Advantages of Joint Theater Support Contracting Command Option:**

(a) Decreases the likelihood of competition for limited local vendor base.

(b) Allows for efficient use of the limited contracting professional staff.

(c) Increases the JFC's ability to establish a baseline for minimal standards for support.

(d) Increases the JFC's ability to standardize the acquisition process.

(e) Allows the JFC to have better visibility of the overall contracting effort.

(f) Increases the JFC's ability to link contracting support to the civil-military aspects of the OPLAN.

(4) **Disadvantages of Joint Theater Support Contracting Command Option:**

(a) Will require implementing new C2 relationships.

(b) May initially decrease the trust of the supported units.

(c) Will require the development of a JMD.

(d) Will generally require an increase in the number of HQ staff personnel needed.

(e) Services' contracting officers may not be familiar with policies and procedures of the joint command.

See Appendix F, "Notional Lead Service and Joint Theater Support Contracting Command Organizations," *for more details on joint theater support contracting command organizational structure.*

FUTURE ORGANIZATIONAL OPTION

To comply with Congressional mandates in National Defense Authorization Act (NDAA) 2007 and NDAA 2008, the Secretary of Defense has called for the establishment of an organization under the auspices of Assistant Deputy Under Secretary of Defense (Program Support) which will provide program management for joint contingency acquisition across the combatant commands and US interagency, during combat operations, post-conflict operations, and contingency operations. The organization will be called the Joint Contingency Acquisition Support Office, headed by a flag officer or Senior Executive Service civilian. An initial operational capability will be established by Fiscal Year 2009 and further expanded in doctrine.

8. Contract Support Integration Planning and Execution

a. **General.** The use of contracted support in military operations must be addressed early on in the planning cycle. Making this happen can be a challenge to many joint force J-4s due to a lack of acquisition officers on their staff, the myriad of contracting options, and the wide variety of contracting authorities. It is imperative the GCC J-4 includes both theater support and external support contract planners in the joint planning process and ensures the contracting effort is tied closely to the overall logistic plan. In some situations, the GCC may choose to designate a lead Service to lead the planning effort, but it is the JFC's responsibility to ensure that the CSIP is properly incorporated into their OPLAN/OPORD.

b. **Developing the Contract Support Integration Plan.** In all operations where there will be a significant use of contracted support, the supported GCC and their subordinate commanders and staffs must ensure that this support is properly addressed in the appropriate OPLAN/OPORD. Normally, the CSIP is developed by the J-4 contracting personnel, but this effort may be assisted by the lead Service (if a lead Service is designated). Additionally, each Service component should publish its own CSIP seeking integration and unity of effort within the supported GCC's CSIP. Close coordination with J-3, J-5, civil affairs, financial management, and legal support is essential to the development of the CSIP (see Figure III-3 and Appendix E, "Contract Support Integration Planning Considerations and Checklist,").

CONTRACT SUPPORT INTEGRATION PLAN

Contract Support Integration Plan (CSIP) Required Elements:

- Theater support contracting organization responsibilities
- Boards and/or center information
- Operational specific contracting policies and procedures to include Service civil augmentation program, multinational, and host-nation support coordination guidance
- Contract administration services delegations

Other CSIP Elements:

- Identification of major requiring activities
- Information on commercial support capabilities to satisfy requirements
- Guidance on the transition from peace-time contracting support arrangements to contingen cy contracting support
- Identification of interagency support requirements including relationships of Department of Defense (DOD) and non-DOD contracting activities
- Identify logistics required to support the contracting effort to include financial management support, program management support, legal support, translator support, etc.
- Identification of specific force protection, security guidance to include restriction on contracted support by time, phase, location, and/or function.

Figure III-3. Contract Support Integration Plan

(1) **Coordinating Theater Support and External Support Contracting Effort.** It is very important the supported GCC J-4 and subordinate JFC J-4 ensure the annex W synchronizes the integration of all Services', combatant commands', and DOD agencies' contracting efforts to ensure there is not undue competition for the same locally available services, supplies, equipment, and subcontractor employees. Without proper coordination, this competition between CAP and theater support contracts will inevitably drive up the prices of local goods and services and could create shortages.

(2) **Determining Organizational Option.** A key focus of any JFC-level CSIP should be the theater support contracting and CAP organizational structure for the JOA. The

CSIP should describe which theater support organizational structure will be used (i.e., Service support to own troops, lead Service, joint theater support contracting command - or a progression from one to another), the specific C2 relationship of contracting activities in the JOA, and the flow of contracting authority in the JOA. It should clearly describe how the logistic related contracting support fits into the overarching CUL support plan to include synchronization with the JARB or JARB-like processes. The CSIP should also include the requiring activities' roles and responsibilities as they relate to requesting contracted support approved through the JARB process. In all operations, the JFC must consider existing Service component contracting assets and organizations in the operational area and how they might need to evolve in terms of staffing, relationships, organization, and authorities to best meet the changing needs of the joint force. Some of the subordinate JFC contracting goals include:

(a) Meeting the JFC's validated support requirements in the most expeditious and effective manner possible.

(b) Achieving civil-military related objectives.

(c) Filling in gaps in organic military support capabilities.

(d) Maximizing the use of limited local vendor base and existing external support contract arrangements within the operational area.

(e) Eliminating competition for resources among Service components.

(f) Maintaining visibility over all contracts, contracting capabilities, and requirements.

(g) Combining to the maximum extent possible all component requirements in order to achieve the most effective and efficient purchases for the joint force.

(h) Shifting from reliance on cost-plus external support contracts to firm fixed-price theater support contracts as the operational environment permits.

(i) Cultivating local sources to facilitate the shift to local contracts designed to reduce cost and to contribute to the JFC's civil-military objectives.

(j) Ensuring that contracted support is properly synchronized with HNS and multinational support arrangements when available.

(k) Ensuring that the theater support and external support contracting efforts, especially Service CAP actions, are properly synchronized and deconflicted.

(l) Identifying associated CAAF related government support requirements, to include FP and PR, which will need to be captured in the CMP or associated portions of the OPLAN.

(m) Address FP and force health protection aspects of contracted support as it relates to quality control, receipt of and inspection of goods, service contractor personnel restrictions, etc., to reduce force health risks along with risk of sabotage, poisoning, and other terrorist-style actions.

(3) **Understanding the Vendor Base.** Since most theater support contracts are awarded to local vendors, as detailed an understanding of the local populace and economy as possible is instrumental in planning for theater support contracting operations. Planning and execution of theater support contracting must consider issues including, but not limited to: what services and supplies are available locally; what type of transportation network is available to move goods; what will be the security environment within theater; are there warehouses available for storage/centralization of distribution; is the banking system mature enough to pay vendors; is the currency stable enough to pay in local funds; and are there cultural issues with race, religion, or gender?

c. **Contracting Support by Phase of the Operation.** As the operation progresses, contracting support will generally shift based on the operational phase: mobilization; initial deployment; joint reception, staging, onward movement, and integration (RSOI); employment sustainment; and finally, redeployment. These stages of contracting support are generally characterized by the types of items purchased and the types of contracting mechanisms used to support specific force support requirements. These phases include: the deployment, employment, sustainment, and redeployment processes described in JP 3-35, *Deployment and Redeployment Operations*.

(1) **Support During Mobilization and/or Initial Deployment.** This is normally the first 30-45 days of a deployment and is characterized by an extremely high operating tempo, confusion, and controlled chaos. The contingency contracting officer's (CCO's) first priority will be to respond to basic life support requirements including billeting, food service - especially potable water, transportation and equipment rental, ground fuel, laundry and bath services, and refuse and sanitation services. During this phase, CCOs may find themselves in the undesirable position of being the requestor, approving official, certifying officer, and transportation office for deliveries. Detailed planning can preclude some of these additional duties; however, physical limitations on the number of support personnel deployed in the early stages of a contingency will require a high degree of flexibility on the part of the CCO. Contracted support will generally be used to provide basic life support and other selected functions. The actual mix of contracting or other support mechanisms such as HNS will be based on risk, reliability, and availability of these various sources of support. Maximum use of existing "peacetime" contracting arrangements should be considered. It is imperative that prior to the main body deployment, the supported GCC and subordinate JFC should ensure that theater support contracting and CAP management organizations are deployed as part of the advanced echelon so that the contracting officer may set up some required life-support functions. Contracting at this time of the operation is generally focused on expediting contract award. Many of the contracting awards during this phase are accomplished by a paying agent.

(2) **Support to Joint RSOI and Employment of Forces.** During this phase, contracting personnel (military and civilian) and contractor personnel will continue to arrive,

though not necessarily at a rate commensurate with the number of troops to be supported. In major operations, a mix of theater support and external support contracts, including LOGCAP, GCSC, AFCAP, and DLA prime vendor contracts may be extensively utilized. At this time, the J-4, comptroller and other staff, will normally have implemented a formal JARB process, or at least a JARB-like process, that will review and make recommendations for CUL support requirements to include determining the specific source of support and provide prioritization of these requirements to the appropriate organization required to provide this support. During this period, a requirements requisitioning controls process will be established. Theater support contracting efforts will still be heavily involved with the acquisition of basic troop support requirements that are not covered by CAP task orders or other means of support. Contracting should move from the SF 44 to more long-term contracting arrangements such as SF 1449, *Solicitation/Contract/Order for Commercial Items*, or blanket purchase agreements.

(3) **Sustainment.** The sustainment stage of the contracting support covers the period from RSOI until redeployment begins. This stage is characterized by a focus on file documentation, cost reduction, and establishing business efficiencies. At this stage, the contracting officer's role may change from a strict focus on requirements fulfillment to a role of a JFC business advisor. During this stage the JFC should proceed with a deliberate plan of action to attempt to move away from cost-plus award-fee CAP task orders and emergency procurement towards long-term contracts, such as indefinite delivery/indefinite quantity or requirements contracts. Requirements will become more defined and consolidated and the use of performance based contracting methods will be maximized when possible. **The transition of CAP task orders to long-term theater support contacts is dependent on specific mission factors such as threat-level and the availability of reliable, local commercial vendor base. It is also important to note that this transition away from CAP task orders is very manpower intensive and may quickly overtask the JFC's limited theater support contracting capabilities.** At this point in the operation, both theater support and CAP contracting officers and managers should have formal processes and controls in place to ensure accountability for all contractor acquired government owned (CAGO) equipment and government-furnished equipment (GFE); begin settling contractor claims, make arrangements to ensure final payments are made, and develop contract termination procedures. They also should initiate the request for disposition instructions for all CAGO equipment and GFE.

(4) **Redeployment support and contract termination.** At this point in the contingency, long-term business arrangements with contractors should become evident in a transition to either final contract closeout or what would be considered normal peacetime business practices. This phase is characterized by significant pressure and urgency to send the troops home. Typical new requirements include packing, crating and freight services; construction and operation of wash racks for vehicles; and commercial air passenger services if USTRANSCOM is not providing this service. The CCO will be required to terminate and close out existing contracts and orders. Ratifications and claims must be processed to completion. Contracting for life support services and base operations must continue until the last troop leaves. During this stage, both theater support and CAP contracting officers and managers should ensure accountability and begin disposition of CAGO equipment and GFE. When a follow-on force is required, the CCO must prepare

contracts and files for delegation or assignment to the incoming contracting agency. Often, the CCO can expect to be one of the last persons to leave the area. To the extent any contracts remain open at the end of an operation, arrangements should be made to transition them to successor organizations such as permanent organizational elements.

A contracting support planning checklist can be found in Appendix E, "Contract Support Integration Planning Considerations and Checklist."

9. Other Key Contracting Planning and Execution Considerations

a. **General.** There are numerous other contracting planning and execution considerations that must be taken into account by the supported GCC, subordinate JFC, and Service components. These considerations run the gamut from contracting support to multinational operations to support of major interagency-led reconstruction requirements, as well as media and political visibility of decisions about selection of contractors and the actions of contractors once in the operational area. The following text is intended to provide a general discussion on the challenges related to these considerations.

b. **Multinational Support.** Contracting officials must be cognizant of contracting activities other than their own to include joint and multinational organizations. Every effort must be made to share vendor information and, if possible, to establish joint/multinational ordering agreements. By not competing with each other, contracting officers can help ensure fair and reasonable pricing to all joint and coalition partners. Planning for and executing common contracted support in an alliance or a coalition is complicated by the lack of a commonly accepted contracting policy or doctrine. Additionally, even in alliance operations, contracting support is not something for which the contracting forces routinely plan or train.

MULTINATIONAL SUPPORT IN OPERATION ENDURING FREEDOM

In July 2006, Kandahar Air Field base operating contracting support transitioned from a US Army Logistics Civil Augmentation Program task order to North Atlantic Treaty Organization (NATO) Maintenance and Supply Agency (NAMSA) contracting support. This action transitioned the Kandahar Air Field base operating support mission from a lead nation (United States) to a multinational support arrangement. This effort included the first use of NAMSA as an operational command responsible for common contracting capability. Called the provision of Real Life Support Arrangement, this support arrangement was codified in a detailed Memorandum of Agreement (MOA) signed by NAMSA along with the four "stakeholder" nations (Canada, United Kingdom, Netherlands and the US) and the NATO's Joint Force Headquarters, Brunssum. This detailed MOA laid out specific organizational procedures to include funding, method of payments, reports, auditing, etc. for this new support arrangement.

SOURCE: *NATO Real Life Support Arrangement No. 011*

(1) **Lead Nation or Role Specialist Nation Contracting Support.** In most multinational operations, the multinational commander will normally designate a lead nation and/or role specialist nation to provide CUL support to the multinational force. Often, the US will be the lead nation responsible for CUL support to the multinational force and this support may be sourced through a combination of theater support or CAP contracts. Challenges to set up a lead nation or role specialist nation contracting support include, but are not limited to: lack of standard terms and procedures; determining funding arrangements and method of payment (e.g., ACSAs/MLSAs); defining requirements to include developing a restricted item list; and developing common standards of support.

(2) **Transition to Multinational Contracting Organization.** Transition from a lead nation or role specialist nation contracting support methodology may be warranted in some long-term alliance operations. In these situations, planning for such a transition should begin as early as practicable and involve all major troop contributing nations. Key to success is the identification of a competent contracting organization and developing specific contracting agreement as described in Figure III-4.

c. **Interagency Support.** Similar to multinational support, US forces may be required to provide CUL support to both governmental and nongovernmental organizations. In many operations, interagency support may be limited in scope and may not pose a significant challenge to the supported GCC and subordinate JFC; however, in all defense support of civil authorities (DSCA) and some stability operations, this support can be much more significant. This support will be managed IAW contracting organization options discussed in paragraph 6 above. In most cases, a lead Service will provide this support through theater support contracts or CAP task orders or combination of both. Key to success of interagency support is to ensure that CCDR planners, to include the J-4, are aware of and are involved in OGA and NGO planning efforts. Planners must address specific DOD contracting support responsibilities to OGA and NGO operations to include specific OGA and NGO requirements. Coordination channels to the supported OGAs and NGOs must be included early in the planning cycle and included as part of coordination mechanisms, including funding procedures (e.g., Economy Act reimbursement or cite to specific Foreign Assistance Act authority) to manage this support in the operational area.

INTERAGENCY SUPPORT IN OPERATION IRAQI FREEDOM

In Operation IRAQI FREEDOM, the lead Service responsible for common user logistic and contracting support, the Army, was responsible to plan, coordinate, and provide life support for Department of State locations to include both the embassy within the "Green Zone" as well as their provincial reconstruction teams located in various locations in Iraq. Army Central Command utilized its Army Field Support Brigade's Logistics Civil Augmentation Program capabilities.

SOURCE: Army Sustainment Command Briefing

MULTINATIONAL CONTRACTING AGREEMENT REQUIREMENTS

- Lead nation, role specialist nation or shared responsibility arrangements.
- Manning considerations (tour length, contracting certifications, etc.).
- Types of support desired (by country and multinational headquarters).
- Requirements generation and validation procedures.
- Standards of support.
- Administrative cost sharing procedures.
- Operational funding to include billing procedures along with period and method of payments.
- Reporting and oversight procedures.
- Audit authority and procedures.
- Fraud investigations policy and procedures.
- Process for resolving disputes.
- Process to amend the agreement.
- Process to add and terminate countries from the agreement.
- Policies and procedures for providing support to contractor personnel.
- Policy, make-up and procedures for working groups and/or management forums.

Figure III-4. Multinational Contracting Agreement Requirements

See JP 3-08, Interagency, Intergovernmental Organization, and Nongovernmental Organization Coordination During Joint Operations, *and JP 3-28,* Civil Support, *for more information on contracting during interagency and DSCA operations.*

d. **Stability Operations.** Stability operations support USG plans for stability, security, transition, and reconstruction operations and likely will be conducted ICW and in support of host nation (HN) authorities, OGAs, IGOs, and/or NGOs. Contracting support to stability operations can be a tremendous challenge to the supported GCC and subordinate JFC, especially when the mission requires significant contracting support to the Department of State (DOS) to assist in major reconstruction actions and restoration of essential government services. Normally, this reconstruction related contracting effort will be done in support of the chief of mission (COM).

(1) **Civil-Military Impact of Contracting.** Theater support contracting and some external support contracting actions can have a positive, and sometimes negative, effect on the civil-military aspects of the overall OPLAN. Since the majority of theater support contracts are awarded to local vendors; these actions have a tangential benefit by increasing the local vendor base, promoting goodwill with the local populace, and improving the local economic base. In many stability and reconstruction operations, there may be a high degree of local unemployment, which can lead to local unrest and cause local nationals to support an insurgency simply for monetary compensation. Depending on the scale of the contracted support, it can be one of many mechanisms used by the JFC in support of the overall objectives; however, planning and executing these civil-military contracting actions can be very manpower intensive. **If not properly staffed, a lead Service or joint theater support contracting command can be quickly overwhelmed in their dual mission to coordinate both forces support and support to civil-authorities.**

A soldier and an Iraqi contractor discuss a new water purification plant on the Tigris River.

(2) **Program Management Vice Contracting.** A substantial challenge to contracting support to major reconstruction operations is a need for detailed understanding of these requirements that are far different from those normally required for forces support and the ability to translate those requirements into executable work statements, followed

closely by the ability to efficiently manage their execution. These requirements can easily exceed DOD capabilities in the area of skill sets and in shear magnitude of the requirement. In general, deployable DOD contracting officers are trained to provide forces support so they have limited training and experience in major reconstruction actions. **Major reconstruction requires the complete gamut of acquisition professionals, especially those trained in contracting, program management, and requirements definition. These actions are more analogous to major weapon-system acquisition and major military construction (MILCON) actions versus traditional forces support contracting arrangements.** These types of skill sets are very limited within DOD and many of the individuals who possess these skills are not part of the operational force. So, if major reconstruction support requirements are anticipated (normally in support of DOS), the supported GCC and subordinate JFC must make appropriate plans to ensure acquisition personnel with the specialized skill sets necessary to accomplish reconstruction operations are deployed, in addition to the theater-support contracting personnel.

See JP 3-34, Joint Engineer Operations, *for more information on construction related contracting.*

(3) **Assessing and Balancing Risk to Forces Support.** Another major challenge in planning for and executing contracting support in stability operations is balancing the risk to forces support and the potential positive impact on the civil-military aspects of the supported GCC's objectives. What may be good for forces support may not meet the needs of the civil-military aspects of the overall campaign plan. **Transitioning to local vendor support can be accomplished by moving the requirements of a CAP task order to a theater support contract or by setting subcontracting goals within a CAP task order to move from a TCN and/or expatriate work force to a local national work force.** In either case, both the increased security risks and contract management requirements must be closely analyzed prior to making any formal decisions. When contemplating transferring contract work to local sources, **the lead Service or joint theater support contracting command must work closely with the supported GCC, the subordinate JFC, and the Services to assess these risks and make determinations on which contracting support actions can be effectively and safely transferred to local sources and which ones cannot.** It may be wise to begin the transition to local vendor support by starting with low risk, non-mission essential services first, especially if these services could be performed off-base or away from US forces.

(4) **Balancing Contracting Best Business Practices with Operational Needs.** The JFC planners must work closely with the lead Service or joint theater support contracting command personnel to balance acceptable contracting business practices and operational needs. In some cases, a tradeoff process may be appropriate when it may be in the best interests of the USG to award to other than the lowest priced offeror or other than the highest technically rated offeror in order to achieve best value for the government considering other factors such as overall civil-military strategic objectives, schedule, and performance. Examples of such contracting actions follow:

(a) Awarding to a vendor based on civil-military considerations (i.e., the company is owned by or substantially employs local nationals) versus lowest cost.

(b) Developing a PWS or SOW that may require the use of manual labor, in lieu of mechanized equipment, in order to employ more local nationals; even though this may drive the cost up and increase the delivery schedule.

(c) Awarding a contract to a local national vendor versus a lower costing foreign vendor in order to maintain a viable local vendor base.

(5) **Fiscal Authorities.** Contracting support in stability operations requires a careful consideration of the DOD and OGA fiscal authorities and often requires coordination with the COM personnel, as well as a plan to transition from DOD funding to other sources of funding. For example, infrastructure support may transition from DOD funding to an effort financed by the US Agency for International Development.

e. **Homeland Defense and Civil Support Operations.** Planning and executing contracting support to homeland defense and civil support operations has similarities as well as significant differences from planning and executing contracting support in foreign contingencies. For example, utilizing systems support contracts in both homeland defense and civil support operations is similar to utilizing systems support contracts in foreign contingencies except for the fact that the contractor personnel integration challenges may be significantly less due to a lower threat level and less stringent deployment requirements. Theater support of and external support contracting, however, may be very different depending on the type of civil support operations.

HURRICANE KATRINA SUPPORT

On Sept. 9, 2005, Kellogg Brown & Root Services Inc., Arlington, VA., was awarded a $15,000,000 task order under a cost reimbursement, indefinite-delivery/indefinite-quantity construction capabilities contract for recovery efforts in support of the US Army Corps of Engineers response to the immediate aftermath of Hurricane Katrina. The work performed provided for immediate disaster recovery response to repair pumps, restore utilities, and efficiently and rapidly accomplish dewatering activities in the Plaquemines, East and West basins in New Orleans. This task order was issued under the US Navy's Global Contingency Contracting (at the time called the Construction Capabilities Program) managed by the Naval Facilities Engineering Command Atlantic, Norfolk, VA.

SOURCE: Department of Defense Public Affairs Press Release

(1) **DOD Contracting Support in Civil Support Operations.** Normally, as delegated by the Department of Homeland Security, the Federal Emergency Management Agency (FEMA) is the lead federal agency during national incident responses. When required, US Northern Command (USNORTHCOM) will provide DSCA in the 48

contiguous United States, Alaska, and the Virgin Islands and Puerto Rico as directed by the President and/or SecDef. US Southern Command (USSOUTHCOM) and US Pacific Command (USPACOM) have similar responsibilities to support homeland defense and support to civil authority actions in US territories within their respective AORs. Generally, this defense support comes in the form of organic military forces with limited contracted support. The key value of military support in domestic operations is that it deploys as basically self-supporting for logistics, communications, and life support. Key principles related to contracting support in civil support operations follow:

(a) FEMA, not DOD, is the lead federal agency responsible to coordinate contracting support to disaster relief operations. The General Services Administration is the primary federal agency providing additional contracting support to FEMA contracting operations.

(b) DOD does not augment other federal agencies with contracting staff, but can perform specific contracting related tasks as directed by the President or SecDef.

(c) Military forces operating in civil support operations should closely coordinate operations with other federal, state, local, and tribal contracting operations in order to avoid competing with tribal, local, state, and federal agencies for limited local commercial resources.

(2) **Operations Under Title 32 USC.** There are many civil support operations that are conducted at the state level by Army and Air National Guard (NG) units providing military support under state active duty or Title 32 USC authority. When NG units deploy within their states, territories, and possessions, they normally receive contracting support from their home station. In these situations, they will usually have several GPC holders with the unit and, when required, warranted contracting officers from the United States Property and Fiscal Office, Purchasing and Contracting Division. These are generally short term deployments such as disaster response. When the NG has contracting personnel shortages in a particular state, the National Guard Bureau (NGB) will coordinate with other states' NGB contracting offices to provide short-term contracting personnel support augmentation to the state requesting assistance. In some cases, the NGB may also form and dispatch a "contracting tiger team" of experienced contracting personnel that is capable of soliciting, awarding and administering large service and MILCON contracts. At all times, NGB contracting offices have authority to obligate federal funds in support of Active Component forces. Active Component forces may establish support agreements with NGB contracting offices to provide contracting support during homeland defense or DSCA operations.

NATIONAL GUARD CONTRACTING SUPPORT

In the aftermath of hurricane Katrina, the US Property and Fiscal Office, Purchasing and Contracting (USPFO P&C) offices and Air National Guard (ANG) base contracting offices from all over the US provided contracting officers to support Louisiana, Mississippi and other state National Guard units deployed to assist the recovery operations. The ANG Crisis Action Team at Andrews Air Force base, MD fielded requests for additional contracting personnel and deployed ANG contracting personnel where needed. Army National Guard units which road marched to the operational area took with them government purchase card holders and received direct contracting support from their home state USPFO P&C office during their road march and while deployed.

SOURCE: National Guard Bureau, Contracting Office

CHAPTER IV
CONTRACTOR MANAGEMENT

> *"If you try to combine a Soldier and a Merchant in one person, you will labor in vain."*
>
> **Admiral Cornelious Metelieff, 1608**

1. Contractor Control and Management Challenges

a. **Key Differences Between Contracted and Military/DOD Civilian Support.** The management and control of contractor personnel is significantly different than C2 of military members and DOD civilians. **Unlike military members and DOD civilians, contractor personnel are not part of the direct chain-of-command. They are managed and controlled through contractor management and governmental oversight staff IAW the terms and conditions of their contract.** Commanders do not generally have legal authority to direct contractor personnel to perform tasks outside of their contract; however, in emergency situations (e.g., enemy or terrorist actions or natural disaster), the ranking area or base commander may direct CAAF to take FP or emergency response actions not specifically authorized in their contract as long as those actions do not require them to assume inherently governmental responsibilities. While the management and control aspect is unique to this category of the "total force," there are numerous additional risks and challenges that must be dealt with when utilizing contracted vice military support (See Figure IV-I).

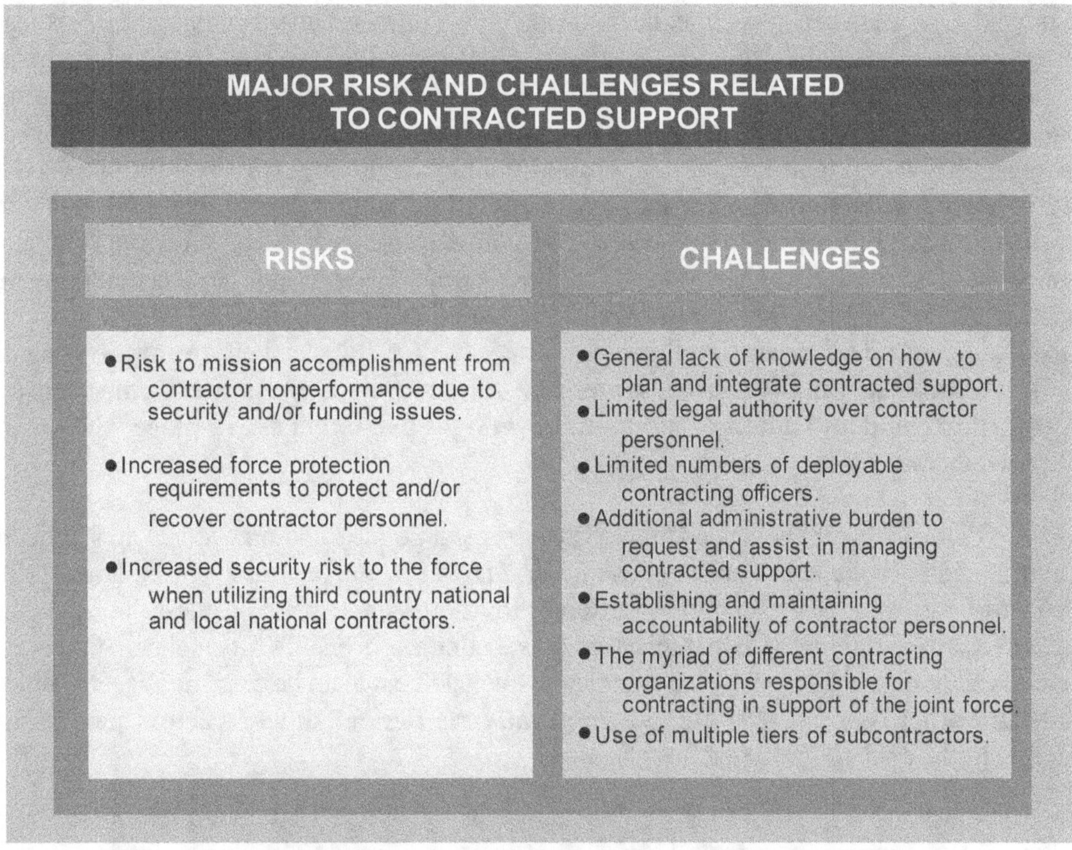

Figure IV-1. Major Risk and Challenges Related to Contracted Support

b. **Providing Proper Military Oversight.** Well planned and deliberate military oversight of contractor personnel in support of military operations is imperative to ensure that contracted support is properly integrated into the operational support structure. Due to the very nature of contracted support, **contractor management is accomplished through a myriad of different requiring activities, CORs, supported units, contracting organizations, and contractor company management personnel, many of which are not under direct JFC C2.** Additionally, contractor management nuances and issues are not well understood by most commanders and staff officers. While specific contractor management policy has been developed, the implementation of such policy is still a significant challenge in most military operations, especially operations in uncertain, hostile, and/or austere environments.

(1) Key to success in this contractor management challenge is for the GCC and subordinate JFCs to establish clear, enforceable, and well understood theater entrance, accountability, FP, and general contractor management policies and procedures early in the planning stages of any military contingency. The supported GCC and subordinate JFCs must work closely with the Service components and combat support agencies to ensure that proper contract and contractor management oversight is in place, preferably well before joint operations commence.

(2) It is important to understand that the terms and conditions of the contract establish the relationship between the military (USG) and the contractor; this relationship does not extend through the contractor supervisor to his employees. **Only the contractor management can directly supervise contractor employees.** The military chain of command exercises management control through the contract management team. This team normally consists of the contracting officer, COR, and the "on-site" contract company manager. In some situations, such as with LOGCAP support, this management team may also include DCMA ACOs and special contract management organizations such as the Army's LOGCAP support unit (LSU). **One of the key challenges for the supported GCC and subordinate JFC is that for many contracts the contracting officer may not even be located within the operational area.** A similar situation is also true for some contractor supervisors and managers. Many small contract companies may not have actual "on-site" supervisors and instead may only have a limited number of managers deployed to the operational area. **This operational reality is why the CORs are such an important part of the contracting management team and the reason commanders must ensure appropriate command administration and oversight personnel are in place when using contracted resources.**

(3) IAW DOD policy, contractor management policies and procedures apply equally to prime and subcontractor personnel at all tiers, however, due to privity of contract, prime contractor has the responsibility to ensure provisions implementing these policies and procedures are disseminated to and followed by subcontractors and their personnel. Of course, this adds additional challenges to the contracting management team because **no direct military contract authority exists over the potential multiple tiers of subcontractors performing services in the operational area.**

(4) In contingency operations, commanders are responsible for ensuring (through their contract management team) that contractors comply with orders, directives, and instructions issued by the GCC and subordinate JFCs, including those relating to FP, security, health, safety, and relations and interaction with local nationals. In circumstances where DOD contractor personnel are authorized to be armed, commanders are responsible for ensuring they comply with specific GCC and subordinate JFC guidance for the operational area, including rules of engagement (ROE) and RUF, use of weapons in self-defense, and local license requirements. Commanders should ensure promulgation of appropriate procedures for arming contract security personnel and investigating use of force incidents. Contractors in contingency operations who commit violations of these may be subject to both the Uniform Code of Military Justice (UCMJ) and the Military Extraterritorial Jurisdiction Act.

DODI 3020.41, Contractor Personnel Authorized to Accompany the US Armed Forces, *provides comprehensive DOD policy on the subject of contractor personnel management in contingency operations. Additionally, CJCS Manual (CJCSM) 3122.03B* Joint Operation Planning and Execution System, *Volume II,* Planning Formats, *provides additional detail on contractor management planning and execution requirements.*

2. Contractor Personnel Legal Status and Discipline

a. **The Hague and Geneva Conventions.** Law of war treaties, such as the Hague and Geneva conventions, attempt to establish and clarify the status of contractor personnel when supporting military operations (See Figure IV-2). These treaties entitle CAAF to be treated as POWs. The 1949 Geneva Convention Relative to the Treatment of Prisoners of War (Article 4) provides that POW status upon capture is extended to, among others, contractor employees, provided that they are authorized to accompany the force and are issued a Geneva Conventions ID Card. During armed conflict with nations that are not signatories to these treaties, the status of contractors may be less clear. Commanders should consult their SJA for legal advice in these situations.

b. **Types of Contractor Employees and Their Legal Status.** As described in Chapter I, DOD contingency contractor employees fall into two primary categories:

(1) **Non-CAAF employees** are employees of commercial entities not authorized CAAF status but who are under contract to DOD to provide a supply or service in the operational area. Non-CAAF include day laborers, delivery personnel, and supply contract workers. **Non-CAAF have no special legal status IAW international conventions or agreements and are legally considered civilians. They may not receive a Geneva Conventions ID card, thus not entitled to POW treatment if captured by forces observing applicable international law.**

(2) **CAAF** are contractor employees who **are specifically authorized through their contract to accompany the force** and have **protected legal status IAW international conventions.** IAW these international conventions, **CAAF are non-combatants, but are entitled to POW status if detained.**

EXCERPTS FROM KEY INTERNATIONAL AGREEMENTS

Hague Convention in 1907 (Article 13)	1949 Geneva Convention Relative to the Treatment of Prisoners of War (Article 4)
"Individuals who follow an army without directly belonging to it, such as...contractors, who fall into the enemy's hands and whom the latter thinks fit to detain, are entitled to be treated as prisoners of war, provided they are in possession of a certificate from the military authorities of the army which they were accompanying."	"Persons who accompany the armed forces without actually being members thereof, such as ...contractors, who fall into the hands of the enemy, and whom the latter think fit to detain, shall be entitled to be treated as prisoners of war, provided they have received authorization from the armed forces which they accompany, who shall provide them for that purpose with an identity card."

Figure IV-2. Excerpts from Key International Agreements

c. **Discipline and Commander's Authority.** Legal jurisdiction and commander's authority over contractor personnel varies depending on contractor personnel nationality, CAAF or non-CAAF designations, operational specific policies, and the type and severity of the discipline infraction. Normally, local national contract employees are subject to local and/or HN laws while US citizens and TCN CAAF may or may not be subject to local and/or HN laws depending on provisions, if any, documented in existing SOFAs or other international agreements. **All CAAF however, are subject to US federal law to include the newly expanded UCMJ jurisdiction as discussed later in this section.** Commanders at all levels must understand that while they do not have full command authority over contractor personnel as they do military members, they do have the authority to direct CAAF in matters of FP and security and play a direct role in maintaining good order and discipline within the military force. So while minor CAAF discipline infractions are normally handled through the contract company management, serious CAAF discipline infractions can and should be, addressed by military and/or Department of Justice channels. To the extent that commanders determine that disciplinary actions may be necessary for CAAF, they should first coordinate their actions with their SJA and government contract management team. This coordination is necessary because of potential jurisdiction issues along with possible impact on contract performance, cost, and government liability as well as determining the appropriate manner to address the situation.

(1) **Host Nation Law.** All non-CAAF are subject to HN law. CAAF are also subject to local laws unless specifically exempted by SOFAs, other international agreements, and in cases where there is no functioning or recognized HN. **HN law, to include transit country law, can directly affect contracting as well as contractor management actions.** The supported GCC, subordinate JFC, and Service components must ascertain how these laws may affect contracted support, to the extent feasible, and consider any limiting factors in both contingency and crisis action operational contract support planning. Service components are responsible to ensure contracting officers take these laws into account as they develop and oversee the execution of contracts. Limiting factors may include workforce and hour restrictions; medical, life, and disability insurance coverage; taxes; customs and duties; cost of living allowances; hardship differentials; and danger pay.

(2) **Status-of-Forces Agreements.** SOFAs are international agreements between two or more governments that address various privileges, immunities, and responsibilities and enumerate the rights and responsibilities of individual members of a deployed force. They can be, although rarely are, used to define CAAF legal status (e.g., the circumstances of HN criminal and civil jurisdiction) as well as contracting related legal obligations (e.g., taxes, customs). When applicable, SOFAs may establish legal obligations independent of contract provisions.

(3) **US Federal Law.** Barring a SOFA or other international agreement, a HN will generally have exclusive jurisdiction over offenses committed within its territory. In the absence of any HN jurisdiction or the exercise of it, US federal law may apply to CAAF misconduct. See Figure IV-3.

APPLICABLE FEDERAL LAWS

- War Crimes Act of 1996 (Title 18 USC, Section 2441)
- Military Extraterritorial Jurisdiction Act of 2000 (Title 18 USC, Section 3261)
- The Uniting and Strengthening America by Providing Appropriate Tools Required to Intercept and Obstruct Terrorism Act of 2001 (Public Law 107-56) (commonly referred to as the USA Patriot Act)
- Federal Criminal Prohibition Against Torture (Title 18 USC, Section 2340)
- Uniform Code of Military Justice as expanded by the National Defense Authorization Act of 2007

Figure IV-3. Applicable Federal Laws

(a) **War Crimes Act of 1996.** Depending on the offense committed, US national CAAF may be prosecuted for war crimes under the War Crimes Act of 1996. This act defines a war crime as any grave breach of the 1949 Geneva Conventions (such as willful killing or torture) or any violation of common Article 3 of the Geneva Conventions. Penalties include fines, imprisonment, or the death penalty if death results to the victim. Prosecutions under the War Crimes Act are the responsibility of federal civilian authorities.

(b) **Military Extraterritorial Jurisdiction Act of 2000.** In November 2000, the Military Extraterritorial Jurisdiction Act of 2000 was passed by Congress and signed into law. This law permits the prosecution in federal court of civilians who, while employed by or accompanying the Armed Forces overseas, commit certain crimes. Generally, the crimes covered are any federal-level criminal offense punishable by imprisonment for more than one year. The law applies to any DOD contractor or subcontractor (at any tier) or their employees provided they are not a national of or a legal resident of the HN. It does not apply to non-DOD contractor employees unless their employment relates to supporting the mission of DOD. This law authorizes DOD law enforcement personnel to arrest suspected offenders IAW applicable international agreements and specifies procedures for the removal of accused individuals to the US. It also authorizes pretrial detention and the appointment of counsel for accused individuals. Like the War Crimes Act, actual prosecutions under the Military Extraterritorial Jurisdiction Act are the responsibility of federal civilian authorities.

DODI 5525.11, Criminal Jurisdiction Over Civilians Employed By or Accompanying the Armed Forces Outside the United States, Certain Service Members, and Former Service Members, *provides more information on the implementation of this law.*

(c) **USA Patriot Act**. In October 2001, the Uniting and Strengthening America by Providing Appropriate Tools Required to Intercept and Obstruct Terrorism (USA Patriot Act) Act of 2001 was passed by Congress and signed into law. The USA Patriot Act was enacted by Congress in response to the September 11, 2001 terrorist attacks. One of its provisions allows the US to apprehend and prosecute US citizens and foreign nationals who commit crimes on overseas US bases and facilities. Similar to the War Crimes and Military Extraterritorial Jurisdiction Acts, prosecutions under the USA Patriot Act are the responsibility of federal civilian authorities.

CONTRACTOR PERSONNEL PROSECUTION

The USA Patriot Act has been successfully used to prosecute a non-DOD US government contractor employee for crimes committed on an overseas US military forward operating base in Afghanistan. The individual in question was convicted of three misdemeanor counts of simple assault and one felony count of assault resulting in bodily injury.

SOURCE: *Jurist: Legal Reviews and Research,* University of Pittsburgh, School of Law, August 2006

(d) **Federal Anti-Torture Statute**. Contractor personnel, such as those serving as military interrogators, could also be prosecuted under the federal anti-torture statute. A person found guilty under the act can be incarcerated for up to 20 years or receive the death penalty if the torture results in the victim's death. Similar to the other federal laws, actual prosecutions under this statute are the responsibility of federal civilian authorities.

(e) **UCMJ**. As expanded by the National Defense Authorization Act of 2007, UCMJ has jurisdiction over persons serving with or accompanying the Armed Forces of the United States in the field, both in times of declared war and during all contingency operations. In accordance with DOD guidance, the unique nature of this extended UCMJ jurisdiction over civilians requires sound management over when, where, and by whom such jurisdiction is exercised. The UCMJ authority over CAAF must be judiciously applied and carefully coordinated with Department of Justice personnel to ensure that the CAAF discipline infractions are handled in a prompt, thorough manner and within the proper legal framework.

d. **Disciplinary Options.** The supported GCC, subordinate JFC, and Service component commanders can address contractor personnel disciplinary issues or misconduct through revocation or suspension of clearances, restriction from installations or facilities, or revocation of privileges. DFARS rules allow the contracting officer to direct the contractor, at its own expense, to remove and replace any contractor employee personnel who jeopardize or interfere with mission accomplishment or who fail to comply with or violate applicable requirements of this clause. The process of removing contractor employees is dependent upon the established GCC policies and the extent to which those policies are incorporated in the terms and conditions of the contract. When confronted with disciplinary problems involving contractors and contractor employees, commanders should seek the assistance of their legal staff, the contracting officer responsible for the contract, and the contractor management personnel. This allows for a thorough review of the situation and a recommendation for a course of action based on the terms and conditions of the contract, applicable international agreements, and HN or US law.

3. Deployment/Redeployment Planning and Preparation

a. **General.** The global nature of the systems and external support contractor base dictates that contractors may deploy CAAF employees and their equipment from anywhere in the world. Even US-based contractors may have personnel originating from foreign locations and/or TCN employees. Proper deployment of contractor CAAF personnel and equipment requires early planning, establishment of clear and concise theater-entrance requirements, and the incorporation of standard deployment related clauses in appropriate contracts.

b. **Contractor Management Planning Overview.** Contractor management planning is related to, but not the same as, contracting support integration planning. While the CSIP is focused on how we will acquire and manage contracted support, contractor management planning is focused on the government obligations under the terms and conditions of the contract to provide support (e.g., accountability, FP, GFE) to contractor personnel. This includes developing policies and procedures required to ensure proper integration of contractor personnel into the military operations. While the JFC-level CSIP is coordinated and written by the J-4 or designated lead Service contracting staff, **there is no single primary or special staff officer responsible to lead the contractor management planning effort.** By its very nature, contractor management integration-related planning responsibilities cross all primary and special staff functional lanes. To address this situation, **the JFC should consider establishing a contractor management integration working group to ensure the various contractor management challenges are addressed and synchronized across all primary and special staff lines.** The JFC's lead Service contracting staff, responsible for contracting and/or joint theater support contracting command personnel, acts as advisors to the subordinate JFC and/or working group on how the contracting process affects in-theater contractor personnel management. The lead service contracting staff should not be designated as the lead for contractor management planning or execution oversight since their role is to assist the appropriate GCC and subordinate JFC staff section as necessary to ensure that the overall contract support effort is properly integrated with the contractor management planning effort. See figure IV-4.

(1) **Contractor Management Plan.** IAW DOD policy, the supported GCC and subordinate JFC must identify operational specific contractor management policies and requirements in the appropriate portion of the OPLAN/OPORD. These requirements include, but are not limited to: restrictions imposed by applicable international and HNS agreements; contractor-related deployment, theater reception, accountability, and strength reporting; operations security plans and restrictions; FP; PR; contractor personnel services

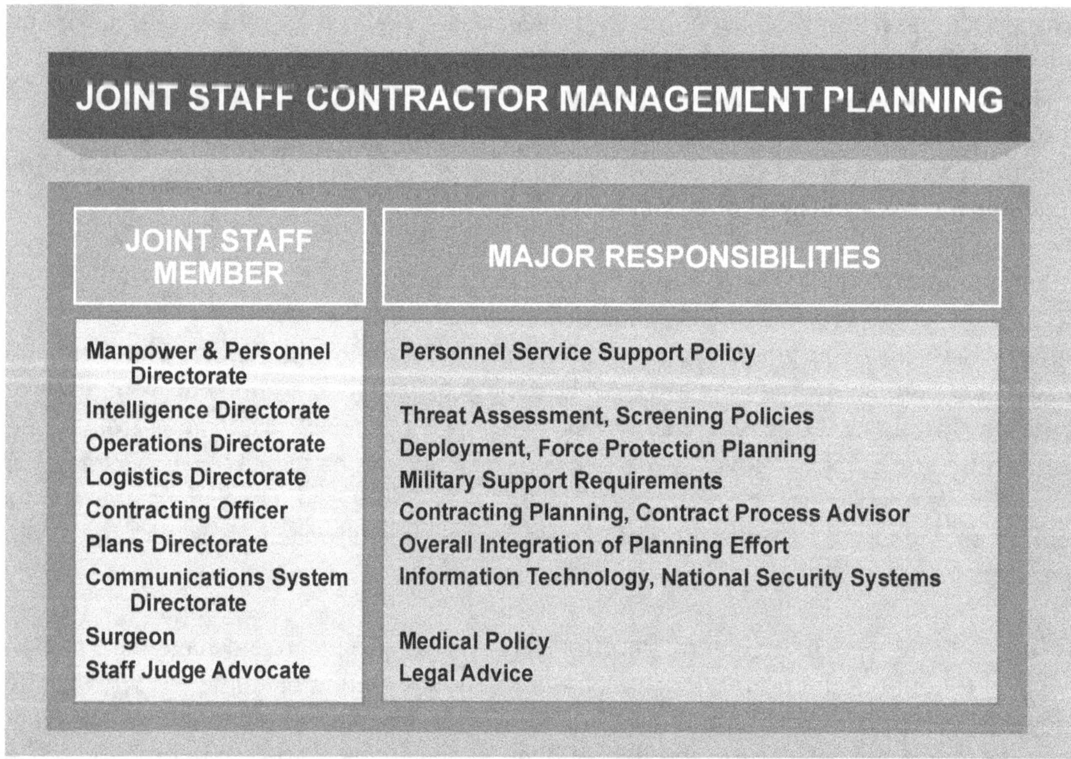

Figure IV-4. Joint Staff Contractor Management Planning

support; medical support; and redeployment requirements. For each operation, the GCC should publish a CMP. The CMP specifies operational specific contractor personnel and equipment requirements in order for the JFC, Service components, joint theater support contracting command (if established), SOF, and DLA to incorporate into applicable contracts as required. The JFC and Service components should prepare supporting CMPs that support the GCC's CMP but provide more specific details.

CJCSM 3122.02C, Joint Operation Planning and Execution System (JOPES) Volume III (Crisis Action Time-Phased Force and Deployment Data Development and Deployment Execution*), DFARS Sub-Part 225.74,* Defense Contractors Outside the United States, and *DFARS PGI 225.7401*, Contracts Requiring Performance or Delivery in a Foreign Country, *provide additional information on the contractor integration planning and procedures.*

(2) **Planning for the Continuation of Essential Contractor Services.** The JFC and all subordinate commanders responsible for coordinating contracted support are required by DOD and CJCS policy to plan for the continuation of essential contractor services during contingency operations. This planning requirement includes, but is not limited to, the following key considerations:

(a) Formally establishing risks associated with the use of contracted support, and when deemed appropriate, taking steps to mitigate these risks.

(b) Identifying mission essential contracted support requirements.

(c) Ensuring all contracts clearly obligate contractors to continue essential contractor services during a contingency operation even in the event of hostile acts.

(d) Having clearly established government and contractor responsibilities to ensure effective FP and security of deployed contractor personnel as dictated by the local threat environment.

(e) Developing specific plans to replace contingency contractor personnel who are performing essential contractor services in contingency operations or to otherwise mitigate their loss of services to include alternative sources (military, DOD civilian, local, national, or other contractor(s)) or other actions that will mitigate the loss of such support.

Refer to DODI 3020.37, Continuation of Essential DOD Contractor Services During Crises, *for more information on this subject.*

(3) **Avoiding Unscrupulous Labor Practices.** The supported GCC, subordinate JFC, and Service component commands must take great care to avoid contractor management related actions that may be construed as trafficking in persons. **Specific concerns in this area include, but are not limited to: illegal confiscation of passports, providing substandard housing, and uncontrolled use of labor brokers (normally through subcontractors) to avoid deployment preparation requirements.** These

practices are clearly against international law, US law, Presidential directives, DOD policies, and military alliance policies and must not be tolerated.

Refer to Victims of Trafficking and Violence Protection Act of 2000, *Department of Defense Directive (DODD) 5500.7-R,* Joint Ethics Regulation, *National Security Presidential Directive (NSPD)-22,* Trafficking in Persons, *and DFARS Clause 252.222-7006,* Combating Trafficking in Persons, *for more information this subject.*

c. **Linking Contractor Management Requirements to the Contracting Process.** The PCO is responsible to incorporate contractor management policy and procedural requirements into the contract. **The ACO and/or the supported unit CORs are the links to the PCO for the oversight of contract performance and contractor management policy and procedure compliance.** For prearranged contracted support, the PCO will use standard DFARS deployment clauses to ensure that the contractors understand and are prepared to execute their contract in a contingency environment. While generic in nature, these clauses ensure that contractors understand and comply with basic deployment preparation and in-theater management requirements. For contracts let for specific operations, the PCO should address theater and other operational specific contract requirements specified by the COR and subordinate JFC in the PWS, operational specific contract clauses, and other terms and conditions of the contract. The process for establishing contractor employee status and for ensuring that operational specific requirements are met by all CAAF is discussed in detail later on in this chapter.

d. **Determining Contractor Status.** PCOs, utilizing DOD policy and ICW guidance from the requiring activity, determine contingency contractor employee status up front in the contracting process. For many employees, determining their status is relatively simple; for others, it is not. The key to success is for the contracting officer to be familiar with and follow DOD contractor management policy including applicable DFARS guidance and specific theater requirements. This determination should be made in close coordination with the supporting legal office.

(1) The key factors that determine the specific status of a contractor employee are area of performance (normal proximity to US forces), citizenship, place of hire, normal place of residence, and place of residence in the operational area. For example, all US citizens employed under a systems support contract or subcontract that requires the service to be performed in support of deployed equipment, will, IAW DOD policy, be automatically afforded CAAF status. Likewise, all TCN contractor and subcontractor employees who do not normally reside in the operational area should be afforded CAAF status. In some cases, mission essential local national contractor personnel who work in the vicinity of US forces and are required to reside with US forces may be afforded CAAF status. A good example of a local national CAAF would be an interpreter who has a habitual relationship with a supported unit. It is imperative that the PCO and requiring activities be aware of the appropriate DOD policy and GCC contractor management guidance when determining the contingency contractor personnel status of TCN and local national personnel.

(2) CAAF status will be formally codified by the issuance of a Geneva Convention Card (either a hard copy DD Form 489 or common access card [CAC]) and an LOA that reflects the appropriate level of government provided support (mess; billeting; post/base exchange access; morale, welfare, and recreation (MWR) access; medical care; etc.) when deployed. The GCC must be prepared to address issues that arise related to contractor employee status and/or in-theater support. In major operations that have significant contracted support, it may be necessary to establish a joint contractor personnel integration working group responsible for researching and providing recommended solutions to the myriad of contractor personnel issues that may arise when planning and executing joint operations. This working group would act as the adjudication authority for contractor personnel support related issues and would be made up of joint force primary and specific staff members as required.

e. **Establishing Theater Entrance Requirements.** The supported GCC, ICW the appropriate subordinate JFC and Service components, determines and publicizes operational specific theater entrance requirements for all CAAF hired outside the JOA. Local national CAAF will receive appropriate training, equipment, etc., as required by GCC policy when hired. Theater entrance requirements include, but are not limited to, operational or JOA specific administrative preparation, medical preparation, as well as general training, and equipping guidance.

Overarching DOD policy on theater entrance requirements can be found in DODI 3020.41, Contractor Personnel Authorized to Accompany the US Armed Forces. *This policy document also provides a comprehensive list of other related DOD, CJCS, and Service policy documents. Additionally, operational specific contractor management requirements are found in DFARS Sub-Part 225.74,* Defense Contractors Outside the United States.

f. **General Overview of Specific Theater Entrance Requirements.** The following is a synopsis of the key theater administrative and entrance requirements that can and will impact the joint force and Service components. The supported GCC and subordinate JFC staffs should work closely with the Service component staffs, special operations units, and other organizations as required to ensure that they understand, promulgate, and enforce these theater entrance requirements.

(1) **Identification Cards.** All CAAF are required by international law to be issued a Geneva Conventions ID Card. The military departments are responsible to ensure that CAAF receive a DD Form 489 Geneva Conventions ID Card and/or a CAC prior to beginning deployment to the operational area. Expiration dates on the DD 489 and CAC should correspond to the end date of the contract period of performance. Normally, only replacement cards will be issued in the operational area.

For additional guidance, see JP 1-0, Personnel Support to Joint Operations. *See DODI 1000.13*, Identification (ID) Cards for Members of the Uniformed Services, Their Dependents, and Other Eligible Individuals, *DODD 8190.3*, Smart Card Technology, *and the appropriate Service regulation for more information on issuance of personal identification cards to contractor personnel.*

(2) **Letters of Authorization.** An LOA is required for CAAF to process through a deployment center; to travel to, from, and within the operational area. LOAs contain specific dates to cover the deployment and are issued to the contactor personnel prior to arrival in the operational area. Additionally, the LOAs identify any additional authorizations and government-furnished support CAAF (to include local nationals designated as CAAF) are entitled to under the contract. The PCO, or designee, shall validate requirements for and availability of, government support at the deployment center, joint reception center (JRC), and within the operational area with the requiring activity prior to preparing the final solicitation package and prior to preparing the LOA. Any change in the contract dates or entitlements will result in an updated LOA being issued to the contractor. CAAF are required by policy to maintain a copy of their LOA and have it in their possession at all times.

DOD policy on LOA requirements can be found in DODI 3020.41, Contractor Personnel Authorized to Accompany the US Armed Forces.

(3) **Security Screening/Biometrics Identification Card/Base Access.** Currently, there is no standard methodology for screening and issuing base access security badges for contractor personnel. The JFC must ensure that local screening and security badge issuance policy and procedures are in place for all contractor employees requiring access. This requirement is especially pertinent to contractors who have not been issued a CAC. Related PWSs and subsequent contracts should include the requirement that non-CAAF requiring base access participate in the local command's screening and vetting program as a condition of employment.

See DODI 2000.16, DOD Antiterrorism (AT) Standards, *for policy on screening contractor employees.*

(4) **Medical Preparation**. The medical preparation of CAAF includes deployment health briefings, medical surveillance screening, medical and dental evaluations, deoxyribonucleic acid specimen collection, determining prescription and eyeware needs, and immunizations. Specific medical related theater entrance requirements, such as human immunodeficiency virus screening requirements, are established by the supported GCC staff surgeon in consultation with the subordinate joint force surgeons. This medical related theater guidance normally covers specific immunization requirements, restrictions applicable to certain TCN or local national personnel, for specific mission functions (e.g., food service workers). Dental conditions that may preclude medical clearance include lack of a dental exam within the last 12 months or required dental treatment or re-evaluation for oral conditions, which are likely to result in dental emergencies. Service components and their associated contract management organizations are responsible to ensure CAAF meet predeployment medical processing and screening requirements.

Additional medical screening and evaluation guidance can be found in DODI 3020.41, Contractor Personnel Authorized to Accompany the US Armed Forces; *DODD 6490.02E,* Comprehensive Health Surveillance; *DODI 6490.03*, Deployment Health; *DODI 6205.4,*

Immunization of Other Than US Forces (OTUSF) for Biological Warfare Defense; and *JP 4-02*, Health Service Support.

(5) **Protective Clothing and Uniforms.** Normally, contractors are responsible to ensure their employees are outfitted with appropriate occupational specific protective clothing and equipment necessary to safely carry out their contract requirements. Service components are responsible to ensure CAAF have adequate military protective clothing and equipment specified in the contract, to include any individual GFE items, IAW the supported GCC directives and Service policies. Normally, contractor personnel will not be issued or wear regulation US Service uniforms and/or other uniform items; however, the GCC or designated subordinate can authorize certain contractor employees to wear standard US Service uniforms on an operational need basis. In these cases, the uniform should be readily distinguishable through the use of distinctive patches, arm bands, nametags, and/or headgear. Contractor personnel authorized to wear distinctive military uniforms are required by policy to carry written authorization for the wearing of said uniforms on them at all times.

(6) **Special Training Requirements for Contractor Personnel**. The Services, DOD agencies, USTRANSCOM, and USSOCOM are responsible to ensure that current DOD required standard training and any operational-specific JFC and Service mandated training is accomplished prior to deployment of contractor personnel into the operational area. Key contractor personnel training requirements include, but are not limited to:

(a) Legal status familiarization to ensure all contractor personnel understand their legal status IAW international law to include prevention of human trafficking information (required for all CAAF).

(b) Familiarization training on US laws, HN laws, and SOFAs that contractor personnel may be subject to (required for all CAAF).

(c) Government-furnished support familiarization that informs contractor personnel of what authorized government-furnished support (postal, MWR, medical, etc.) is available to them while accompanying US forces.

(d) Law of war training commensurate with their duties and responsibilities. Specific training should include, but is not limited to, Geneva Conventions enemy prisoner of war (EPW) training for all contractor personnel who may come in contact with EPWs or other detainees and RUF training for all contractor personnel performing armed security services.

(e) Personnel recovery training to inform contractors of the processes and actions required should they become isolated (required for CAAF). This training includes individual survival, evasion, resistance, and escape training as determined by the requiring activity and supported GCC, the subordinate JFC, and the Service component.

(f) Medical awareness training related to local health risks, medical related policies and procedures (required for all CAAF).

(g) Theater specific requirements to include specific FP and security, hazard awareness to include local commander's authority, wear and use of military protective gear (if issued), compliance with theater deployment and redeployment accountability standards and requirements, and related information, such as customs and religious awareness training, as determined by the supported GCC, subordinate JFC, or Service component commander (required for all CAAF as directed by subordinate JFCs and Service component commanders; may include in-theater briefings to non-CAAF whose area of performance is on a US base or in the immediate vicinity of US forces).

Along with DODI 3020.41, Contractor Personnel Authorized to Accompany the US Armed Forces, *other key reference documents for contractor training include: FAR Part 22.17*, Combating Trafficking in Persons; *DODD 2310.2,* Personnel Recovery; *DODD 2311.01E,* DOD Law of War Program; *DODI 1300.23,* Isolated Personnel Training for DOD Civilian and Contractors; *DODI 6490.03*, Deployment Health; *JP 1-0*, Personnel Support in Joint Operations; and *JP 4-02*, Health Service Support.

g. **Contractor Personnel Certification and Deployment.** Service and SOF component commanders and heads of DOD combat support agencies, field activities, and other organizations are responsible to ensure that their CAAF being deployed into an operational area are properly certified and fully integrated into the supported GCC and subordinate JFC deployment planning process. There are several different CAAF certification and deployment methodologies.

(1) **Process and Deploy With the Supported Unit.** This is the preferred method of deployment for CAAF who have a habitual relationship with a specific supported unit. This group deployment process involves certification and deployment of CAAF in a coordinated fashion between the supported unit, contracting officer, the contractor and, if applicable, any contractor management oversight entity such as the Army's LSU. Once certified, these CAAF normally deploy as part of the supported unit, which provides time-phased force and deployment data.

(2) **Process and Deploy Non-Unit Related Personnel.** Non-unit related personnel (NURP) include CAAF who deploy as individuals or as part of a small group and not with any habitually supported unit. CAAF NURP are required to deploy through a replacement center or equivalent Service certified or operated individual deployment preparation process. In this process, CAAF NURP are certified for deployment via their processing through a designated replacement center or the equivalent process. Once certified, CAAF NURP are generally immediately deployed via transportation means directed by military authorities or as identified in their contracts. In-processing through the JRC in theater is required.

(3) **Self-Certification and/or Deployment.** Self-certification and/or deployment applies to CAAF who have authorization for self-certification and/or deployment. **This**

authorization is usually restricted to major contractors such as Service CAP contractors and is granted by the appropriate Service. CAAF self-certification must meet or exceed replacement center processing and preparation standards. In some cases, selected contractors may also be authorized to arrange their own overseas deployment as long as it is properly integrated into the Defense Transportation System. Self-certifying and self-deploying contractors are still required to meet CAAF accountability standards as set by DOD and/or CCDR policies.

See DODD 4515.13-R, Air Transportation Eligibility, *for more information.*

PREPARATION AND DEPLOYMENT OF CONTRACTOR PESONNEL

In Operation IRAQI FREEDOM, Kellogg Brown & Root, Inc. (KBR), the prime Army Logistics Civil Augmentation Program (LOGCAP) contractor, was authorized by the Department of the Army to self-certify its personnel for deployment. To meet this requirement, KBR set up and operated its own replacement center for its direct hire employees. KBR's replacement center was inspected and certified by Army officials to ensure that it met Service individual deployment processing requirements. Additionally, KBR was given authorization by the supported commander to arrange deployment of its employees through commercial means. In this and in other earlier operations, KBR utilized commercial air carriers to fly in both prime and subcontractor personnel directly to major airbases, thus freeing up military transport aircraft to perform other more high priority missions.

SOURCE: Department of the Army G-4 LOGCAP Program Manager

h. **Time-Phased Force and Deployment Data.** CAAF being deployed into the operational area must be properly integrated into the deployment process. This is especially important in uncertain or hostile environments where there is limited or no commercial access to the operational area. In these types of operations, time phased force and deployment data should include contractor NURP cargo and employee requirements.

i. **General Redeployment Considerations.** Service components, DOD agencies, USTRANSCOM, and USSOCOM are responsible to ensure that redeploying CAAF are properly managed and controlled. Key redeployment actions include, but are not limited to: updating the appropriate contractor employee accountability database; recovery of government issued badges and ID cards; recovery of all GFE or CAGO equipment; required debriefings; and, withdrawal of security clearances (as applicable). Out-processing through the JRC in theater is required. Paragraph 6 provides more discussion on GFE and CAGO.

j. **Medical Redeployment Requirements.** CAAF are required by DOD policy to complete a post-deployment health assessment and obtain a post-deployment health debriefing. Contract terms and conditions should clearly identify these responsibilities, including allocating all associated cost.

4. In-Theater Contractor Management

In-theater contractor management challenges discussed in this section include accountability, reception, on-ward movement, and restrictions on contractor support (by area, phase of operation, or other measures as appropriate). Other key in-theater contractor personnel management considerations such as discipline, FP, and security, are discussed in other sections of this chapter.

a. **Personnel Accountability.** Proper accountability of CAAF is extremely important to the GCC. Without such information, it is impossible to properly plan for and to integrate contingency contractor personnel into the overall operation. It is critically important in determining and resourcing government support requirements such as facilities, life support, FP, PR, MWR, and force health protection in uncertain, hostile, and/or austere operational environments. All contracting agencies are required by DOD policy to ensure that CAAF data is entered and maintained in the DOD designated contractor personnel management system of record. This system will provide the supported GCC and subordinate JFC by-name accountability of CAAF when deployed into an operational area to include personnel predeployment certification and location data.

b. **Reception.** All CAAF will be processed in and out of the operational area through a JRC or other personnel centers designated by the supported GCC. The JFC can establish additional in-and-out processing requirements for their operational area. The JRC will verify that the CAAF are included in the contractor personnel management system database and that the CAAF have met all theater entrance requirements. CAAF who do not meet established theater entrance requirements will either be sent back to their point of origin or placed in a holding area until these requirements are met. The supported GCC will establish specific policies for handling CAAF who do not meet all established theater entrance requirements which their subordinate JFCs will implement.

c. **Onward Movement.** Once the JRC or comparable organization fully verifies that the CAAF are included in the contractor personnel management system database and that all theater entrance requirements are met, CAAF are eligible to be issued any required operational specific identification documents. If required by the contract, the JRC operations/movement cell or the respective contractor management team will arrange for transportation of the contractor and their equipment to the point of performance. Arrangement of intratheater transportation of CAAF will include the appropriate FP/security measures commensurate with FP/security measures taken for DOD civilians.

d. **Location and Movement Considerations.** Contractors can be expected to perform virtually anywhere in the operational area, subject to the terms of the contract, and the JFC's risk assessment of the local threat level. **Based on this risk assessment, the supported GCC and/or subordinate JFCs may place specific restrictions on locations and timing of contract support; however, care must be taken to coordinate any restrictions with component commanders, applicable DOD agencies, and contracting officers to avoid disruption of planned operations and potential unauthorized commitment of US funds through contract constructive changes.** Additionally, contractor personnel location reporting and equipment movement must be incorporated into the supported GCC and subordinate JFC movement control, personnel accountability, and FP plans. See below for more information on FP related requirements.

5. Force Protection and Security

FP and security of contractor personnel and equipment is a shared responsibility between the contractor and the government. In a permissive environment, the supported GCC and subordinate JFC may have only limited special planning considerations and this security responsibility would normally fall to the contractor. In hostile environments, contractor related FP and security requirements can be a major challenge to the JFC and subordinate commands. Additionally, FP of CAAF is a significant consideration for the supported GCC.

a. **Determining Specific FP and Security Measures.** The GCC and subordinate commands at all appropriate levels must plan for the protection of CAAF in the overall FP and security plan in operations where the contractor cannot obtain effective security services, such services are unavailable at a reasonable cost, or threat conditions necessitate security through military means. In general, **military provided FP is the preferred option for operations where there is an on-going or anticipated level II (small-scale, irregular forces conducting unconventional war) or III (conventional forces capable of air, land, or sea attacks) threat level**. In these situations, it is in the best interest of the Government to provide military security to CAAF or at a minimum, closely coordinate the use of commercial security firms to protect CAAF.

See DODI 3040.21, Contractor Personnel Authorized to Accompany the US Armed Forces, *JP 3-10,* Joint Security Operations in Theater, *and JP 3-07.2,* Antiterrorism, *for more information on determining specific FP and security measures.*

b. **Establishing Force Protection/Security Requirements in the Contract**. The contracting officer shall include in the contract the level of protection to be provided to CAAF. In appropriate cases, the JFC may be required to provide this security through military means, specific security measures shall be mission and situation dependent as determined by the subordinate JFC. **All contingency contractor personnel, not just CAAF, whose area of performance is in the vicinity of US forces shall be required to comply with applicable supported GCC and subordinate JFC FP policies and procedures.** In hostile environments CAAF, living with and routinely working within a US military facility or in direct vicinity of US forces, will receive security measures commensurate with the level of security provided to DOD civilians. Non-CAAF employees whose area of performance may be on a military facility or in close contact with US forces will receive security support incidental to their work location.

c. **Base Access.** The JFC and individual base commanders are responsible for the security of all military facilities within the operational area. The lack of a fully fielded DOD-wide standard security and badging system requires the JFC and subordinate commanders to develop local policies and procedures to vet and badge CAAF as well as those non-CAAF who need routine access to military facilities. Not having these policies and procedures in place can severely reduce the effectiveness, timeliness, flexibility, and/or efficiency of contracted support. This can be an especially significant issue when changes to the operation require a quick surge of contracted support from one base to another. Often local badging policies preclude this from happening in a timely manner.

Contracted "jingle trucks" were used extensively to deliver non-mission critical supplies to military forces in Afghanistan.

d. **Individual Movement Protection.** Another key concern for the JFC is protection of contractor personnel during individual or small group movements within the operational area. In general, **all CAAF should be provided protection during transit within the operational area commensurate to protection provided to DOD civilians.** It is important that the JFC and subordinate commanders balance FP requirements with the need for contractor personnel to have ready access to their place of performance. Overly restrictive movement requirements can hinder the responsiveness of contracted support, especially for systems support contractors who are providing support on an area or general support basis. Too lenient movement restrictions may have a negative effect on contracted support if contractor personnel become casualties due to the lack of/or improper enforcement of movement related FP and security measures. In operations where more than a level I (Negligible) threat exists, routine military movements should include contractor personnel. Otherwise, commanders responsible for local FP and requiring activities well need to make special arrangements. In all cases, contractor movement protection/security arrangements must be coordinated with the designated movement control organization.

e. **Convoy Protection.** The subordinate JFC or lead Service component responsible for land movement control must establish, publish, and implement operational specific contractor related convoy FP standards and procedures. Depending on the operational situation, contractor vehicles and personnel may be required to join military convoys (commonly referred to as a mixed "green" and "white" convoy) or they may be authorized to transit the operational area in convoys made up exclusively of contractor personnel and vehicles (commonly referred to as an all "white" convoy). In either case, the JFC or designated subordinate commanders are responsible to ensure that adequate FP measures are in place to protect contractor convoy operations that are in support of the deployed military forces.

See the Air, Land, Sea Application Center's Multi-Service Publication Army Field Manual 4-01.45/ Marine Corps Reference Publication 4-11.3H/ US Navy Tactics, Techniques, and Procedures 4-01.3/US Air Force Tactics, Techniques and Procedures (I) 3-2.58, Multi-Service Tactics, Techniques and Procedures for Tactical Convoy Operations, *for more information on integrating contractor personnel into convoy operations.*

f. **Issuance of Personal Defense Weapons.** In general, individual contractor personnel should only be armed in exceptional circumstances. However, consistent with applicable US, HN, international laws, relevant SOFAs or other international agreements, and DOD policy, the supported GCC may authorize contractor personnel to carry a government issued or approved individual weapon for personal protection. Variables such as the nature of the operation, the type of conflict, any applicable status agreement related to the presence of US forces, and the nature of the activity being protected require case-by-case determinations. IAW DOD policy, the supported GCC can delegate this authority down to a designated general officer, normally the subordinate joint force joint security officer.

DODI 3020.41, Contractor Personnel Authorized to Accompany the US Armed Forces, *provides detailed policy guidance on issuance of personal defense weapons to contractor personnel.*

g. **Use of Contingency Contractor Personnel to Provide Security Services.** If consistent with applicable US, HN, international laws, and relevant SOFAs, a defense contractor may be authorized to provide security services for other than uniquely military functions. **The supported GCC and subordinate JFC should, however, use caution when contemplating the use of contracted security to protect US forces, facilities, and supplies in any operation where there is a current or expected level II or III threat.** In general, threat levels above level I (Negligible) require significant FP measures (e.g., crew served weapons, combined arms response, indirect fire) that may be considered to be an inherently governmental function.

(1) Whether a particular use of contract security to protect military assets is permissible is dependent on the facts and requires detailed legal analysis and coordination by the subordinate JFC and SJA. Variables such as the nature of the threat, the type of conflict, applicable HN laws, and the nature of the activity being protected require case-by-case determinations. The use of force by contingency contractor personnel is often strictly limited

by domestic (HN and US) laws and not protected by SOFA provisions. Contingency contractor personnel, providing security services who exceed the limits imposed by applicable law, may be subject to prosecution. Additionally, there can be significant civil-military related risks when utilizing private security forces in military operations. For example, the local populace may not distinguish between a private security guard and a US military member when it comes to use of force, improper actions, etc. Incidents involving private security forces can have potentially negative impact on the operation, especially since the supported GCC and their subordinate JFC have significantly less direct control on these private security contractors when compared to US military members.

(2) The supported GCC, subordinate JFC, and/or designated subordinate Service or functional component commanders must ensure that operational specific procedures to coordinate contractor provided security and military security/FP support actions (to include incident reporting and investigation) are developed, promulgated, and enforced within the operational area. Additionally, the supported GCC and subordinate JFC must work closely with the contracting officers, the contractors, the HN (if applicable), and DOS in establishing appropriate RUF for contract security companies operating in the operational area.

Supported GCCs, their subordinate JFCs, and their legal staffs should closely review provisions found in *DODI 3020.41*, Contractor Personnel Authorized to Accompany the US Armed Forces, *and DODI 1100.22,* Guidance for Determining Workforce Mix, *when contemplating the possibility of utilizing commercial security services to protect US forces, facilities, and supplies.*

h. **Reporting Law of War Violations.** All DOD personnel are required to report possible, suspected, or alleged law of war violations. Additionally, CAAF are also required to report such incidents to their requiring activity or to the CCDR. The supported GCC, subordinate JFC, and Service component commanders, especially when utilizing armed contract security, should ensure that adequate coordination mechanisms are in place to ensure timely and accurate law of war incident reporting.

DODD 2311.01E, DOD Law of War Program, *provides detailed policy guidance on law of war incident reporting.*

6. Government Provided Support

As most military operations are conducted in austere and/or hostile and uncertain environments, contractor personnel support will often be provided through military means or via another contract directed by the military. **In these situations, the contracting officer will detail the government support to be provided in the terms and conditions of the contract, after determining support requirements and availability of such support from theater DOD support providers.** Planning and oversight of government furnished support actions is primarily a Service component responsibility; however, in major operations, this support planning and execution may require direct involvement of the supported GCC and subordinate JFC. Without understanding the overall support requirements, to include specific government furnished support requirements for CAAF, the supported GCC and subordinate JFC will not be able to accurately plan for and direct CUL support responsibilities in the operational area. Key areas of concern are discussed below in more detail along with major references for areas of support.

a. **Base Operating Support (BOS) and/or Facilities.** In permissive and non-austere operations, contractors should arrange for their own lodging, subsistence, and facilities; however, in austere and/or hostile and uncertain environments this may not be practical or desirable. The circumstances under which the military provides this support would be those in which the contractor has no commercial infrastructure from which to draw from or when the cost for a contractor to furnish the support is not economical. In situations when contractor-arranged BOS would impede the government's efforts to provide FP, generate competition with the military, or adversely influence prices, the military must consider providing the support or at least directly coordinating this support to be within US bases. The supported GCC and subordinate JFC have the authority to direct where CAAF reside, within the terms and conditions of the contract. CAAF must generally be provided the same standard support that is applied to DOD civilian personnel of similar grade and responsibility level.

(1) In some operations or phases of operations, selected CAAF may be required to temporarily live under field conditions. Field conditions are quite different from normal civilian life and are characterized by austere and communal living and a collective responsibility for the living area. **Contracting officers should ensure that there is appropriate language in the contract for CAAF who are expected to perform their duties in field conditions.**

(2) Subsistence may be provided to contractors, either in conjunction with government-provided lodging, or separately, when contractor employees during their daily work shift are unable to obtain subsistence for operational reasons. For those CAAF living in field conditions, the food provided might be prepackaged rations with very little opportunity for choice; consequently, special diets may not be accommodated. In some sustained operations, it may be desirable to have separate contract run CAAF dining facilities that provide ethnic based subsistence that may be both less expensive and more appealing to TCN and/or local national CAAF.

(3) Although it is natural to expect reimbursement from contractors for the cost of lodging and subsistence, the cost for such support would normally be included in the overall cost of the contract. Therefore, when possible, subsistence support should be done on a non-reimbursable basis, eliminating the unnecessary administrative burden of reimbursement. However, joint force and Service component planners must include the cost of supporting contractors in the overall cost of the operation so that adequate funding is provided.

(4) Like BOS, facility support to contractor personnel is very situationally dependent. Facilities support must be planned for as early on as possible, especially in austere and/or hostile and uncertain environments where contract companies cannot coordinate their own facility support. In these situations, external and systems support contractor managers must provide their requirements during contract negotiations. The

contracting officer or designated ACO must then coordinate these requirements with the appropriate joint force or Service component staff engineer. In some situations, theater support contracts which utilize TCN CAAF vice local national non-CAAF employees may also require government furnished base operating and facilities support.

b. **Personnel Recovery.** PR is the sum of military, diplomatic, and civil efforts to prepare for and execute the recovery and reintegration of isolated personnel. The GCC and subordinate commands must plan for the possible isolation, capture or detention of CAAF by adversarial organizations or governments. Recovery of isolated personnel may occur through military action, action by NGOs, other USG-approved action, and diplomatic initiatives, or through any combination of these options. IAW DOD policy, all US citizen CAAF must be included in the PR program as demonstrated in JOPES and subordinate OPLANs and OPORDs, as well as CMPs. The supported GCC and subordinate JFC may designate that certain other CAAF are included in the PR program as well. The contract and CMP should address how contractors are included in the theater PR plan and receive PR training and support products.

DODI 3020.41, Contractor Personnel Authorized to Accompany the US Armed Forces; *DODD 2310.*2, Personnel Recovery; *and JP 3-50,* Personnel Recovery, *provide additional details on the PR program.*

c. **Individual Protective Equipment.** The contract shall specify the level of government-furnished support and what support is reimbursable to the government. Generally, contractors shall be required to provide all life, mission, and administrative support to its employees necessary to perform the contract according to DODI 4161.2, *Management, Control, and Disposal of Government Property in the Possession of Contractors.* However, when determined necessary by the Service component commander IAW the supported GCC and subordinate JFC guidance, CAAF may be issued military individual protective equipment (e.g., chemical defensive gear, body armor, personal protective equipment) at no cost to the contractor.

d. **Medical.** During contingency operations in austere and/or hostile and uncertain environments, CAAF will most likely be unable to access medical support from local sources. The DOD policy requires the supported GCC and subordinate JFC to provide emergency medical care to contractor employees, including CAAF and non-CAAF who are injured in the immediate vicinity of US forces or on a US base. This medical support includes emergency and resuscitative care, stabilization, hospitalization at medical treatment facilities, and assistance with patient movement in emergencies where loss of life, limb or eyesight could occur. When DOD policy allows and contract terms and conditions require it, the joint force needs to be prepared to provide primary medical care to all CAAF as coordinated by the joint force surgeon, contracting officer, and SJA as mission dictates. All costs associated with the treatment and transportation of contractor personnel to the selected civilian facility are reimbursable to the USG and shall be the responsibility of the contingency contractor personnel, their employer, or their health insurance provider.

Much more detailed guidance on medical support to deployed contractor personnel can be found in DODI 3020.41, Contractor Personnel Authorized to Accompany the US Armed Forces, *DODI 6490.03,* Deployment Health *and JP 4-02*, Health Service Support.

e. **Major Equipment Items.** Major equipment items include Class VII GFE and CAGO equipment. GFE includes Class VII items that are either deployed into the operational area with the contractor or theater provided equipment that is issued to the contractor in the operational area. GFE issuance, maintenance, and return are the responsibility of the appropriate Service component, SOF organization, or DLA contracting organization. However, **in some operational situations, OSD may require the subordinated JFC to coordinate operations/theater specific disposition of GFE and/or CAGO equipment.** For example, in some stability operations, OSD may direct that certain GFE and/or CAGO equipment be transferred to HN or designated multinational force. If transfer of GFE and/or CAGO equipment is anticipated, the subordinate JFC J-4 should work closely with the appropriate DOS, DOD, and affected component organization to ensure that clearly understood and properly coordinated disposition instructions are provided in a timely manner.

f. **Postal.** The nationality of the contractor employee usually determines postal support. US CAAF who deploy in support of US Armed Forces, may be authorized use of the Military Postal Service (MPS) if there is no US postal service available and if MPS use is not precluded by the terms of any international or HN agreement. CAAF TCN employees normally are provided with postal support through the existing HN system or through arrangements made by the employing contractor. In some operations, TCN personnel may be authorized limited access to MPS for the purpose of mailing paychecks to their home country. In most circumstances, TCN and local national employees will not be provided access to the MPS.

Additional information on postal operations can be found in DOD 4525.6-M, Department of Defense Postal Manual.

g. **Mortuary Affairs.** The joint mortuary affairs program is a broadly based military program that provides for the necessary care and disposition of deceased personnel, including personal effects across the full range of military operations. The supported GCC, normally through the Army component acting as the lead Service for mortuary affairs, executes this program in the AOR. This program includes the search, recovery, tentative identification, care, and evacuation or temporary interment, disinterment, and reinterment of deceased personnel, to include all CAAF, within the operational area. Mortuary affairs support to contractor personnel is normally accomplished through USD(P&R) coordination with DOS to include cost reimbursement, where appropriate. The specific nature and extent of the support is determined during the planning process and communicated to military forces and contractors through governing OPLANs/OPORDs and contractual documents.

Additional information on mortuary affairs can be found in DODD 1300.22, Mortuary Affairs Policy *and JP 4-06*, Mortuary Affairs in Joint Operations.

h. **Post/Base Exchange Privileges.** When deployed, CAAF CAC holders are generally eligible to use military exchange facilities for health and comfort items in operations where CAAF do not have access to similar commercial sources. This privilege depends on the overall operational situation, SOFAs, and individual contract terms and conditions.

Additional information on exchange privileges for deployed contractors can be found in DODI 1330.21, Armed Services Exchange Regulations.

i. **Morale, Welfare, and Recreation.** In general, contractors have a responsibility to provide MWR and other quality-of-life support to their own employees as much as practical. The availability of MWR programs in the operational area vary with the deployment location. Available MWR activities may include self-directed recreation (e.g., issue of sports equipment), entertainment ICW the United Services Organization and the Armed Forces Professional Entertainment Office, military clubs, unit lounges, and some types of rest centers. The subordinate JFC should authorize CAAF CAC holders to utilize MWR support on a space-available basis when contractor and/or other sources are not available.

7. Coordinating Non-Department of Defense Contract Support

a. **Scope of Challenge.** The scope of non-DOD contract support integration requirements are very much mission dependent. In some joint operations, the JFC may have only limited requirements to integrate non-DOD contracted support into military operations while in others, there may be major challenges that defy any simple solutions. For example, in OIF, contractors in support of OGAs, IGOs, and NGOs could be found throughout the JOA to include significant use of contracted security forces.

b. **Specific Challenges.** In complex, long-term stability operations, there are a myriad of challenges related to OGA, IGO, and NGO contractors. Key to addressing these requirements is an active civil-military coordination effort to include the use of civil-military operations centers or other mechanisms to ensure proper civil-military information sharing and cooperation. Two of the biggest challenges for the JFC are coordinating non-DOD contractor movements and non-DOD contracted security elements.

(1) **Movement Coordination/Deconfliction of Non-DOD Contractor Personnel and Equipment.** The subordinate JFC may be required to assist in integrating non-DOD contractor personnel and equipment into both air and surface movements, especially during on-going major reconstruction and transition to civil authority related actions. While presenting a planning challenge, it is in the best interest of the subordinate JFC to assist DOS and other non-DOD organizations in contract-related actions within the JOA. The major challenges associated with this support include obtaining advance knowledge of the requirement, determining military responsibility for FP and security requirements, and establishing communications with the contractor.

(2) **Coordination and Support to Non-DOD Private Security Company Operations.** Of all of the non-DOD contracting related coordination tasks, none is more important and challenging than coordinating with non-DOD agencies who hire private

security firms. These private security firms, sometimes including contracted uniformed foreign military members, are routinely used to provide protection of non-DOD personnel in transit and at work sites in high threat areas. Without proper coordination the risk of an incident involving friendly military forces on contractor employees can be significant. The subordinate JFC and its subordinate commanders must take great care in establishing adequate visibility (location, mission, RUF) of these non-DOD private security related contracts. Some key considerations follow:

(a) Does the subordinate JFC have back-up security support requirements to DOS or other non-DOD organizations? If so, are these organizations using private security firms for protection?

(b) What is the subordinate JFC's authority, if any, in planning and utilization of non-DOD contracted security firms?

(c) Where are these security firms operating?

(d) What are the RUF? Did the subordinate JFC have input to the RUF?

(e) Has the JFC, COM, and other interested parties developed workable and reliable information sharing mechanisms? How will the military forces communicate with these private security firms? Are their systems compatible with the on-hand military systems? Has the communication plan been exercised?

(f) Are subordinate commanders properly informed of their local requirements? Have they conducted proper coordination with these security firms and/or rehearsed back-up security actions?

COORDINATING INTERAGENCY SECURITY CONTRACTORS

In Operation IRAQI FREEDOM, Multinational Force-Iraq coordinated directly with the Department of State (DOS) Chief of Mission to ensure that major DOS sponsored reconstruction efforts, to include DOS funded contracted security forces, were properly integrated into military security plans. In this particular operation, the problem was so challenging that combined DOS-Department of Defense coordination center was stood up to provide the necessary planning capabilities, information sharing, and coordination measures. This effort included regional reconstruction coordination centers that were directly linked into area commander's operations centers. These regional coordination centers provided the area commanders key information on DOS missions being performed within their area of operations. This information was critically important when area commander was called on to provide back-up security support to DOS missions, facilities and personnel.

SOURCE: *Private Warriors,* Public Broadcasting Frontline

Intentionally Blank

APPENDIX A
SERVICES' SYSTEMS SUPPORT CONTRACT OVERVIEW

1. General

a. Systems support contracts are prearranged contracts awarded by Service acquisition PM offices that provide technical support, maintenance support, and in some cases, Class IX support for selected military weapon and support systems. Systems support contracts routinely provide support to newly fielded aircraft, land combat vehicles, automated C2, as well as other support systems. Systems support contracting, contract management, and PM authority resides with the Service systems acquisition program offices. Systems support contractor personnel, made up mostly of US citizens, provide support in garrison and often deploy with the force in both training exercises and during contingency operations. Since the supported GCC and subordinate JFC do not maintain resident systems support contracting authority and acquisition oversight, they **generally have less control over the execution of systems support contracts in the JOA than other types of contracts.**

b. Systems support contract FSRs provide key technical support for Service equipment in various locations within the operational area. These FSRs are mission essential CAAF that provide either temporary support during the initial fielding of a system, sometimes called interim contracted support, or long term support for selected materiel systems, often referred to as contractor logistic support. These mission essential personnel are managed by Service acquisition offices and must be properly integrated in to military operations as discussed in Chapter IV, "Contractor Management." The following paragraphs provide an overview of how each Service manages their systems support contracts and associated CAAF.

2. US Army Support

a. The Army uses systems support contracts to support numerous deployable Army systems. Supported systems include, but are not limited to, newly or partially fielded vehicles, weapon systems, aircraft, C2 systems, standard Army management information systems, and numerous communications systems. These prearranged contracts are awarded by the combined Assistant Secretary of the Army for Acquisition, Logistics and Technology (ASA[ALT]), and/or USAMC life cycle management commands (LCMCs) and other independent ASA(ALT) PM offices. In many cases, these CAAF systems support contract personnel have a habitual relationship with the supported unit and provide support both in garrison and upon deployment. These LCMC teams can range from a single LCMC systems contract FSR, such as a combined arms battalion with tanks, to the significant LCMC team presence currently found in the Stryker brigade. When utilized in contingency operations, these contracts and their associated personnel are managed under teaming arrangements between the supported units and the Army's primary acquisition, logistics, and technology (ALT) oversight unit, the Army field support brigade (AFSB).

b. All AFSBs are assigned to ASC, but operate under the OPCON of the regionally aligned Army theater sustainment commands during contingency operations. As the primary ALT support integrator for deployed Army forces (ARFOR), the AFSBs provide systems contract and associated CAAF oversight through their subordinate logistic support elements and brigade logistic support teams. The AFSBs assist the supported units in FSR deployment and function as a conduit between the supported unit and the supporting LCMC and independent Army PM offices.

c. The three LCMCs are USAMC major subordinate commands that include imbedded ASA(ALT) PM offices. These commands are responsible to provide "cradle-to-grave" equipment support from procurement and fielding through sustainment and disposition. LCMCs are a key source for AFSB reach-back and call-forward systems support contract capabilities.

More detailed discussion on Army systems contract support can be found in Field Manual (FM) Interim 4-93.41, Army Field Support Brigade, *and FM 3-100.21,* Contractors on the Battlefield.

3. US Navy - Marine Corps Support

a. The Assistant Secretary of the Navy for Research, Development, and Acquisition (ASN[RD&A]) is the Department of the Navy Acquisition Executive (NAE). The NAE has full responsibility for all acquisition programs through program executive officers (PEOs) and/or project managers or systems command (SYSCOM) commanders. The Navy SYSCOM commanders act for and exercise the authority of the NAE to directly supervise management of assigned programs and report directly to the ASN(RD&A) for all matters pertaining to acquisition. Common responsibilities for these commanders include serving as HCA for both assigned programs and project manager programs and overseeing in-service support of weapon and informational/technical systems. Navy systems support contracts can therefore be awarded by any of the SYSCOMs for their specific types of systems under their responsibility.

b. **The Marine Corps Systems Command (MARCORSYSCOM)** is one of the Department of the Navy SYSCOMs and develops and supports Marine air-ground task force (MAGTF) specific systems requirements to include Marine Corps unique chemical, biological, radiological, and nuclear defense materials and equipment; training systems and equipment associated with Marine Corps unique requirements; amphibious raid; and ground reconnaissance systems and equipment. The MARCORSYSCOM is responsible to develop and support Marine Corps unique ammunition and weapons, to include procurement, surveillance, and maintenance of associated ordnance items.

c. **The Naval Supply Systems Command (NAVSUPSYSCOM) commander** acts for and exercises the authority of the NAE to directly supervise, manage, and serve as the logistics support authority in support of other Navy SYSCOMs, PEOs/project managers, and their assigned acquisition programs throughout their life-cycle. The commander of NAVSUPSYSCOM reports to ASN(RD&A) for overall execution of responsibilities, but also reports to Chief of Naval Operations and the Commandant of the Marine Corps respectively for the execution of in-service logistics support authority responsibilities.

4. US Air Force Support

a. All Air Force systems support contracting is organized under Air Force Materiel Command (AFMC), headquartered at Wright-Patterson Air Force Base (AFB), OH. AFMC is further organized into the Air Force Research Laboratory (AFRL), six product centers, three test centers, and three logistics centers. The AFRL, located at Wright-Patterson AFB, leverages technical information to lead the discovery, development, and integration of affordable warfighting technologies for our air and space forces.

b. The product centers are tasked to develop, design, and acquire the best, most technically advanced weapon systems in the world. The test centers subject each weapon system and its components to exacting operational standards. The logistics centers provide "cradle-to-grave" management, specialized logistics support, maintenance, and distribution for weapons systems worldwide.

Intentionally Blank

APPENDIX B
SERVICES' EXTERNAL SUPPORT CONTRACT OVERVIEW

1. General

External support contracts are prearranged contracts, or contracts awarded during the contingency, from contracting organizations whose contracting authority does not derive directly from the theater support contracting HCAs or from systems support contracting activities. External support contracts provide a variety of logistic and other non-combat related services. This appendix provides high level details regarding key Service and DLA external support contract capabilities. The Service CAPs are the most commonly and extensively used external support contracts. CAPs provide the supported GCC and subordinate JFC an alternative source for meeting logistic services and general engineering shortfalls when military, HNS, multinational, and theater support contract sources are not available or not adequate to meet the joint force needs. All three military departments have their own CAPs, each with some similarities as well as some unique differences.

a. Service CAP similarities:

(1) All serve as an augmentation capability to organic military capabilities.

(2) All are long-term (four to nine years depending on the program) competitively awarded contracts.

(3) All use, or can opt to use, cost-plus award-fee indefinite delivery/indefinite quantity (ID/IQ) task orders.

(4) All potentially compete for the same general commercial support base.

b. Service CAP differences:

(1) Authorized expenditure limit.

(2) Support focus:

(a) LOGCAP focuses on general logistic support and minor construction support. The program utilizes separate support (planning and program support) and performance (task order execution) contracts.

(b) AFCAP focuses on both construction and general logistic services and can be also used for supply support.

(c) GCCC focuses exclusively on facility construction support.

(d) GSCS focuses on facilities support.

(3) Planning and management capabilities.

2. Air Force Contract Augmentation Program

a. **General.** The AFCAP is a worldwide contingency contract tool available to support the Air Force and joint force along with any USG agency in need of urgent logistic assistance in support of contingency operations. AFCAP, like all CAP programs, is designed to rapidly leverage private industry capabilities as a force multiplier in supplying highly responsive solutions to meet global mission objectives across the full range of military operations. The AFCAP contractors have a worldwide capability, coupled with an existing breadth and depth of commercial business interests aligned to be able to meet the contingency operations requirements. Unlike the other Service CAPs, AFCAP can be utilized to procure and expeditiously ship just-in-time commodities. Depending on urgency, degree of requirements definition, or task stability, AFCAP can be tailored into firm-fixed-price, cost-plus-fixed-fee, or cost-plus-award-fee task orders as necessary to best match the government's needs.

b. **Capabilities.** AFCAP is able to provide, as a minimum, 72 core general engineer and other logistic services along with commodity procurement and shipment capabilities. The scope of the AFCAP contract requires that the contractors provide the personnel, equipment, materials, services, travel, and all other means necessary to provide a quick response, worldwide planning, and deployment capability. The contract provides additional capabilities to allow military missions to continue when there are facility or service support constraints. The AFCAP contractors can provide manpower to complete or augment tasks, full range of just-in-time logistics (acquisitions, deliveries, procurement of commercial off-the-shelf items, heavy equipment, leases, bulk materials, war reserve materiel augmentation, etc.), and expedient design/build construction. Whenever possible, the AFCAP contractor draws upon significant in-place location expertise and worldwide commercial vendors with readily available assets. A major contributing effort for AFCAP is in the area of sustainment and maintenance of the deployed forces and initial force projection effort. AFCAP can also be utilized to provide initial joint force beddown of non-Air Force personnel (the Air Force has organic military capability for its own life support). AFCAP may be utilized to help transition and upgrade bare bases from initial austere support standard to temporary-standard facilities and utilities. This allows for the recovery and reconstitution of critical war reserve materiel resources for use at other locations or to support additional expansion for a specific mission. Finally, AFCAP can also provide general equipment support, but is not intended to be used for in-depth equipment maintenance or depot-level overhaul, at contingency locations, since the Air Force already has other provisions for these requirements.

c. **Planning.** AFCAP contractors can be asked to provide rough orders of magnitude (ROMs), however, most ROMs are accomplished by HQ Air Force Civil Engineering Support Agency (AFCESA) staff. AFCAP planning task orders can be awarded to assist customers with their requirement.

d. **Management.** HQ AFCESA provides PM functions, and Air Education and Training Command (AETC) provides contracting support for AFCAP requiring activities. HQ AFCESA is located at Tyndall AFB, FL, with PM deployed forward as required. The AFCAP PCO normally delegates all appropriate contract administration and audit services functions to DCMA IAW the specific needs of that task order. DCMA will provide ACO support, to include monitoring/reviewing/approving the contractor's accounting, purchasing and estimating systems. They also provide property administration and quality assurance support as required. DCMA ACOs also have the authority to execute no-cost change orders to task orders. Should DCMA experience a short-fall for field support during the execution of AFCAP, AFCESA will provide field assessment surveillance teams (FASTs). The AFCESA FASTs are based on a tailorable, multifunctional deployable team concept as needed by task order/location and region – providing oversight, ensuring cost, schedule, and quality task order performance by the AFCAP contractors. AETC will retain all contracting functions not delegated to DCMA, to include all PCO functions (issuance of all task orders), execution of modifications resulting in price changes to task orders, and execution of modifications to the basic contract (exercise of options, etc.).

3. US Navy Global Contingency Contracts

The Navy has two CAP contracts: the GCCC and the GCSC. The GCCC is focused on construction while the GCSC is focused on facilities support. They are both described in more detail below.

a. **GCCC.** The GCCC is a competitively solicited multiple award, cost reimbursable contract with award fee. This acquisition vehicle will provide three pre-qualified sources to provide up to a maximum of $1 billion of construction over five years. The contract provides construction, design/build construction, and related engineering services in response to natural disasters, humanitarian assistance, conflict, or projects with similar characteristics. This includes occasional projects to ensure readiness to perform during emergency situations and military exercises. GCCC is also an acquisition tool that Naval Facilities Engineering Command (NAVFAC) utilizes to support roles for contingency construction outlined in DODD 4270.5, *Lead Design and Construction Agent*.

(1) **Capabilities.** The GCCC, through the Navy, will provide on behalf of DOD, or other Federal agencies when authorized, an immediate response for civilian construction capability. The scope includes the capability to provide general mobilization services for personnel, equipment, and material in support of naval construction forces (NCFs) mobilization and similar mobilization efforts, and to set up and operate material liaison offices at a deployed site in support of NCF operations. Work is predominately construction, however, services incidental to the construction may also be included. Construction critical response during an emergency will primarily support aid for natural disasters, military conflict, or humanitarian aid.

(2) **Planning.** By contract, each contractor is required to maintain an in-place contingency response plan available to facilitate response to emerging requirements. The plan identifies pre-positioned resources, suppliers, and procedures for rapidly developing, detailed execution plans tailored to the specific requirements of the emergency situation.

(3) **Management**. The GCCC is managed by the Naval Facilities Engineering Command, Atlantic in Norfolk, VA. Other NAVFAC components may also be given ordering office authority under this contract.

b. **GCSC.** The Navy's GCSC is an ID/IQ cost-plus award fee contract designed to quickly provide short term facilities support services with incidental construction at various locations (including remote locations) throughout the world.

(1) **Capabilities.** This performance based contract is designed to respond to natural disasters, humanitarian efforts, or contingencies or other requirements such as nonperformance by an incumbent contractor or instances where there is an unanticipated lapse in service. The contract has a capacity of $450 million over five years.

(2) **Planning.** By contract, the contractor is required to maintain an in-place contingency response plan available to facilitate response to emerging requirements. Plan identifies pre-positioned resources, suppliers, and procedures for rapidly developing, detailed execution plans tailored to the specific requirements of the emergency situation.

(3) **Management**. The GCSC is managed by the Naval Facilities Engineering Pacific. Other NAVFAC components may also be given ordering office authority under this contract.

4. Logistics Civil Augmentation Program

a. **General.** LOGCAP is designed to provide general logistics and minor construction support to deployed Army, joint, and multinational forces. The LOGCAP has been routinely used with significant success in supporting full spectrum operations for over a decade. The Army is currently on its fourth contract iteration of LOGCAP. LOGCAP IV differs from LOGCAP I-III in that instead of just one contractor, it now has separate support and performance contractors. More specifically, the Army has selected one support contract and multiple separate performance contractors. Under the LOGCAP IV program, the support contractor conducts the planning and program support. Once the Army has identified a LOGCAP requirement, the support contractor will provide the plan to the performance contractors, receive the proposals from the performance contractors for the task order, evaluate the proposals, and recommend a contractor to execute the plan.

b. **Capabilities.** In general, LOGCAP can be utilized to provide logistic services and minor construction support for any scale operation. Assuming that the support contractor has received sufficient time in advance to coordinate ROM, the technical evaluation plan, and appropriate transportation into the JOA, LOGCAP task orders can be utilized to provide basic life support for up to 77K personnel within 30 days of the announced C-date. LOGCAP is designed for initial force deployment and employment support, it is not intended to be utilized for long-term sustainment support. It is Headquarters, Department of the Army (HQDA) policy that all of the LOGCAP task orders be designed to be readily converted to competitive theater support contracts.

c. **Planning.** The LOGCAP IV planning requirement calls for the LOGCAP support contractor, ICW the supporting contracting support brigade (CSB), to prepare a variety of Army component and joint force-level support plans. The support contractor will prepare and maintain two types of plans; worldwide and focused. Worldwide plans are the contingency plans that generate generic and regional LOGCAP plans for supported commander, normally the Army component-level. These generic plans provide the baseline for contractor support and differentiate between support in a developed country and that required to support a deployment in a nondeveloped area. Focused planning begins with the identification of a specific mission in the crisis action planning process. These specific plans provide a detailed description of equipment, material, personnel and supporting services, facilities, and potential suppliers required to support the customer identified augmentation requirements. The planning contractor also maintains database support for five broad categories: facilities, supplies, services, maintenance, and transportation. Support for actual operations is tailored based on the concept of support developed for the operation.

d. **Management.** The Army LOGCAP is a HQDA program. The HQDA G-4 is the LOGCAP policy and program manager while the USAMC, through its subordinate commands, is responsible for program planning and execution. When required, the Army will deploy a team LOGCAP-forward consisting of a LOGCAP deputy program manager, planning team, and an LSU section, to assist the JFC and ARFOR commander by providing a single focal point for centrally managing LOGCAP execution. Within the operational area, team LOGCAP-forward, ICW the supporting CSB, is responsible for incorporating LOGCAP requirements into OPLANs and/or FRAGORDs and to provide assistance to requiring activities with validating LOGCAP requirements. Once delegated by the ACC PCO, the DCMA will provide ACOs to administer the task orders IAW the base contract and guidance from the LOGCAP deputy program manager. DCMA will also provide quality assurance representatives and property administrators as needed. Units will be required to provide COR support where LOGCAP support is utilized.

5. US Navy Fleet Husbanding Contracts

a. **General.** The Navy maintains a worldwide network of contracts to support US Navy ship visits in foreign ports. The contracts, some of which are regional (multi-nation), country-wide, or port specific, are maintained by the Navy's fleet and industrial supply centers (FISCs), which are aligned to major fleet and GCCs' AORs. Many of the contracts contain provisions to provide basic service and materiel support for small-scale military operations or humanitarian assistance/disaster relief missions. US Navy contracting officers are authorized to order supplies and services from priced schedules. Other services and joint organizations must contact the applicable FISC prior to placing orders for permission to utilize these contract vehicles.

b. **Capabilities.** These fixed priced contracts contain pricing schedules for ship support services and many contain specific clauses and pricing schedules for contingency support items to include providing basic sustainment and materiel support. In addition, husbanding support contractors will likely speak the local language, have in-depth knowledge of the local business environment and may be able to suggest initial sources of supply. In some cases, the husbanding contractor may be able to provide pre-staged material such as vehicles, cell phones, lodging arrangements/tents, etc in advance of advance echelon teams.

c. **Planning.** Primary purpose of fleet husbanding support contracts is to provide support services for ship visits. Consequently, advance notice to contractors and the applicable FISC is required. Husbanding service contracts are an ideal means of obtaining initial support for a small scale, short duration operation; however, transition to more suitable contracting vehicles is necessary should the scope or duration of an operation change.

d. **Management.** Fleet husbanding support contracts are managed by AOR, with alignment of FISCs corresponding to the following AORs: FISC Norfolk maintains contracts for support of USNORTHCOM and USSOUTHCOM operations; FISC Sigonella maintains contracts for support of US European Command, US African Command, and US Central Command operation; while FISC Yokosuka maintains contracts for support of USPACOM operations. Planners should contact the appropriate FISC to determine whether Navy fleet husbanding support contracts may be available to support operations in a particular location. Initial orders on the contract must be placed through the applicable FISC contracting office.

6. Defense Logistics Agency Contingency Contracting Functions and Capabilities

a. **General.**

(1) DLA is DOD's combat support agency providing virtually every consumable item the US military requires, at home and abroad. DLA provides effective and efficient worldwide logistics support to the military departments and the combatant commands under conditions of peace and war, as well as to other DOD components and federal agencies, and when authorized by law, state and local government organizations, foreign governments, and IGOs. DLA's mission includes managing over five million consumable items, processing more than 30 million annual distribution actions, and administering over $900 billion of DOD and other agency contracts. DLA functions as an integral element of the military logistics system.

(2) DLA has been formally designated by the Deputy Secretary of Defense as the DOD Executive Agent for the following commodities: subsistence (Class I); bulk fuel (Class III); construction and barrier materiel (Class IV); and medical materiel (Class VIII). To execute these logistics responsibilities, DLA developed a network of supplier and supply chain relationships, constantly refining contracted support requirements and contract surge clauses that can be accessed to support increased demands. Using a myriad of acquisition strategies such as prime vendor, long-term contracting, and direct vendor delivery to obtain products and services, DLA manages suppliers and entire supply chains, constantly adjusting processes and services and extending capabilities as far forward as needed to sustain the CCDRs and Services. These efforts directly support DOD's increased emphasis on "jointness."

b. **Functions and Capabilities.**

(1) To successfully perform this mission, DLA has developed significant contracting capabilities. Using a variety of contracting mechanisms, partnering arrangements, and forward deployed resources, DLA has the ability to award contracts quickly and effectively. DLA also uses long-term contracts to create efficiencies, working closely with industry to communicate requirements. DLA employs surge clauses to increase flexibility to meet planned or unplanned demands for items or services. DLA manages relationships with thousands of contractors employing global capabilities in supply chains extending around the globe. DLA's use of contracted support to contingency operations has allowed military services to apply resources elsewhere, contributing to increased combat power.

(2) DLA meets the needs of the military departments and other authorized customers by conducting, directing, supervising, or controlling all procurement activities regarding property, supplies, and services assigned to DLA for procurement IAW applicable laws, DOD regulations, the FAR, the DFARS, and the Defense Logistics Acquisition Directive. To the extent that any law or executive order specifically limits the exercise of such authority to persons at the secretarial level, such authority is exercised by the USD(AT&L).

(3) DLA works through the CJCS, with the CCDRs, and directly with the Services to consolidate joint and Service requirements for surge and sustainment supplies and services and to execute sourcing and distribution plans, agreements, and contracts to support theater forces. DLA support requirements come from the Joint Staff and the Services. DLA participates in CCDR sponsored contingency planning conferences, developing DLA support plans in support of CCDRs' OPLANs, and OPORDs. During these planning conferences, DLA inserts DLA logistics capabilities into the planning process, providing input to the annex D (Logistics) and annex W (Contract Support Integration Plan). For OPLANs and OPORDs with TPFDD, DLA develops the DLA support plan, providing detailed information on how DLA capabilities will be executed in support of CCDRs' contingencies and crisis operations.

Intentionally Blank

APPENDIX C
SERVICES' THEATER SUPPORT CONTRACTING ORGANIZATIONS AND CAPABILITIES

1. General

Theater support contracting support capabilities differ between military Services. Based on individual mission and organization, each Service has its own approach to developing, training, and deploying contracting personnel. Although differing in organization, training, and experience, each Service's contracting personnel must meet the Defense Acquisition Workforce Improvement Act certification requirements – including appropriate education, training, and experience. However, knowing the individual Services' organizational approaches, capabilities, strengths, and weaknesses can help the JFC maximize the capabilities provided by each Service.

2. US Army

a. The Army has recently moved to a more integrated approach in its theater support contracting structure. The Army's core of military commissioned officers and noncommissioned officers (NCO) trained as contingency contracting officers are now part of separate, O-6 level CSBs. These CSBs are assigned to the ACC, but are regionally aligned to the existing Army Service component command HQ.

b. The Army's CSBs are made up of contingency contracting battalions, senior contingency contracting teams, and contingency contracting teams. CSB commanders are responsible for training and readiness of their subordinate units. They are also responsible to support, ICW the AFSBs and team LOGCAP-forward, contracting planning efforts at the Army Service component and senior Army logistic command levels.

c. In addition to its uniformed contingency contracting officers and NCOs, the Army has two other methods to supplement the Army's formal contingency contracting force structure: by deploying volunteer military and civilian contracting officers; and, through its emergency essential Department of the Army civilian (EEDAC) program. Military or civilian individuals volunteer to deploy via the Army's G3 Worldwide Individual Augmentation System. EEDAC contracting officers deploy as required based on the level of support required, phase of operation, and local security conditions.

3. US Marine Corps

The Marine Corps has a limited number of uniformed contingency contracting personnel who deploy as part of a MAGTF. The MAGTF contracting section develops a contract support integration plan as part of the overall logistic support plan that includes the number of personnel to be deployed. Generally, the Marine Corps does not deploy civilian contracting professionals in support of contingency operations. Additionally, Marine Corps contracting officers do not contract for construction nor do they possess the necessary skill set to support major reconstruction efforts.

4. US Navy

a. The Navy contingency contracting capability is based on two principles:

(1) The Navy does not maintain a dedicated contingency contracting force. Instead, naval officers and civilians, assigned to field contracting and systems acquisitions commands performing contracting functions, are deployed as contingency contracting officers as operations dictate.

(2) The Navy leverages the network that provides global logistics support to maritime and expeditionary forces operating worldwide to create a scalable and multi-level response to a real world situation.

b. When a CCDR identifies a long-term requirement and obtains the necessary contingency contracting manning via the JMD process, contracting officer billets sourced by the Navy would result in a uniformed contracting officer being assigned as an individual augmentee (IA). IA personnel assignments are currently managed at the Navy-wide level by the Navy Personnel Command. Civilian contracting officers are not utilized in the IA program.

5. US Air Force

a. The Air Force has a very large and well trained theater support contracting capability. The Air Force meets its theater support contracting needs by:

(1) Developing military contracting professionals, enlisted and officer, who typically spend the majority of their career in this field;

(2) Augmenting home-base contracting experience with contingency training and exercises;

(3) Organizing all of its military for potential deployment using flexible, modular skills packages, called unit type codes (UTCs); and

(4) Employing members in a predictable, structured, and managed air expeditionary force deployment process.

b. IAW Air Force policy, military contracting officers spend the majority of their careers gaining expertise through a progression of contracting assignments. Through these assignments military contracting officers hone their skills and become proficient at a wide range of missions in support of their organization. These missions include acquisition and administration of operational support services, construction, and commodities. Additionally, many contracting officers gain experience in logistics and weapon system acquisition. These skills potentially apply to the contracting requirements faced during contingencies.

c. Each Air Force installation supplements base support experience by providing contingency specific training and formal exercises emphasizing the requirements of Air Force FAR Supplement Appendix CC. Operational readiness exercises conducted by wing inspector generals and operational readiness inspectors conducted by major command HQ gauge the unit's ability to perform contingency operations.

d. The Air Force organizes and deploys contingency contracting officers via skill/capability mixes called UTCs. Each UTC specifies a package of capabilities based on the supported population, completion of requisite acquisition professional development program levels, needed equipment number of contracting personnel required and grade restrictions if any. UTCs allow combatant commanders to mobilize a highly modular, flexible contracting force.

e. Each Air Force contracting unit organizes its deployable assets into UTC packages. When a contracting UTC is within the deployment vulnerability window, the Air Force can task UTCs from various units to fill CCDR's specific skill requirements. Although some UTCs have rank requirements (e.g., a requirement for a deployed commander position), the **Air Force contracting UTCs are generally skill based, not rank dependent**. Due to the Air Force's rigid training requirements, the Air Force maintains a large and experienced group of both officer and enlisted contracting officers.

Intentionally Blank

APPENDIX D
DEFENSE CONTRACT MANAGEMENT AGENCY CONTINGENCY FUNCTIONS AND CAPABILITIES

1. Mission

The **Defense Contract Management Agency** is the combat support agency responsible for ensuring major DOD acquisition programs (systems, supplies, and services) are delivered on time, within projected cost or price, and meet performance requirements. DCMA's major role and responsibilities in contingency operations is to provide CCAS to LOGCAP and AFCAP external support contracts, for selected weapons systems support contracts with place of performance in the operational area, and theater support contracts when CCAS is delegated by the PCO.

2. Requesting Support

Service CAP program managers request and coordinate DCMA CCAS support directly with DCMA. All requests for theater support contract delegations will be accepted or declined in writing. Further, any declinations or modifications to delegations will be documented in writing. DCMA may decline a request for CCAS on a case-by-case basis if agency resources are inadequate to accomplish the tasks. For all declinations the Service component or agency awarding activity will assume the declined delegation.

3. Operational Support and Resourcing

a. DCMA provides direct support (DS) to the CCDR through CCAS support teams. CCAS teams may consist of an ACO, quality assurance representative, and property administrator. These teams normally have a DS relationship with LOGCAP and/or AFCAP deployed deputy program managers. In the case of LOGCAP support, the DCMA deployable support team would establish a formal relationship with the Army components' team LOGCAP-forward's deputy program management officer. The DCMA team and its ACOs would collocate as required with the team LOGCAP-forward HQ and subordinate elements as required by the individual operational situation.

b. DCMA uses a risk based resourcing model to provide Title 10, USC contract oversight requirements. During high-risk operations (rapid expansion and consolidation periods) DCMA will provide on-site CCAS support teams providing direct contract oversight. During moderate to low risk continuing operations (post camp build out to start of camp consolidation) DCMA will provide regional CCAS teams providing indirect contract oversight. DCMA will continuously review DOD's resource requirements and make adjustments based on risk assessments using DCMA's contingency operations resourcing model.

4. Entry Criteria

DCMA will provide contract administration oversight capability within 72 hours of receipt of: contract delegation for contingency operation from cognizant PCO and, authorization to enter theater on approved JMD or time-phased force and deployment list.

5. Exit Criteria

In coordination with the JFC and the Services, DCMA will exit a contingency operation when:

a. The mission area is no longer declared a contingency operation area or there is an executive order or law downgrading the operation;

b. The supported customer establishes an installation permanent party with an internal contracting organization; or

c. DCMA will transition from CCAS resourcing to an established DCMA Contract Management Office oversight based on reduced risk to the government or reduced operating tempo.

APPENDIX E
CONTRACT SUPPORT INTEGRATION PLANNING CONSIDERATIONS AND CHECKLIST

1. General

Effective contract support planning must be based on a thorough mission analysis that considers not only the demands of the operation, but also the environment under which it will be conducted. This appendix provides an overview of those considerations planners may use to conduct mission analysis when preparing CSIPs at the combatant command level, JFC level, or subordinate command level.

2. Purpose

The following checklist is intended to provide the supported GCC, subordinate JFC, and Service component commanders and staff a broad overview of the type of issues that should be addressed in a CSIP under annex W. This checklist is not intended to be exhaustive. It is intended to serve as a basic guide as to what to think about when preparing, staffing, and publishing a CSIP. Depending on the scale of the contingency operations, some items may not apply.

3. Mission Analysis

Mission analysis, through either the adaptive or crisis action planning process, provides planners with a comprehensive framework of requirements to support an operation. Mission analysis from a contracting support perspective, whether this be the annex W or the CSIP, should as a minimum include the following below considerations.

a. Identifying Contracting Requirements:

(1) Planners often develop a mindset that contracting is inherently a combat service support function. However, contract support for military operations not only includes logistics, but also may include combat support functions such as engineering, intelligence, and signal/communications. In some instances, contractors may also perform security functions.

(2) Review of OPLAN/concept plan (CONPLAN) and consider commander's intent, mission, level of forces deploying, location, and duration of the operation.

b. Determining the Force Mix:

(1) Determine functions that are inherently governmental (e.g., combat, detainee operations, etc.)

(2) Determine the contracting environment:

(a) Specific statutory/regulatory constraints or exemptions that apply to the supported operation.

(b) HN agreements, customs, laws, culture, language, religion, and/or business practices which may impact contracting operations.

(c) Availability of banks/other financial institutions, and financial practices in the HN.

(d) ACSAs/MLSAs which may impact contracting operations.

(e) Availability/suitability of HN infrastructure and commercial vendors to support contract operations.

(3) Availability of US forces, HN and PN forces which may impact upon contract requirements (e.g., addition of HN and PN forces may reduce or expand contract support requirements), or, may expand.

(4) Extent of NGOs, PVOs, IGOs, and OGAs involvement in AOR which may impact upon contract support requirements. Synchronization with these organizations is critical to avoid competition for local resources.

(5) Likelihood of hostile actions to impact upon the continuity of contract support.

(6) Cost considerations. Determining CAP costs versus theater support contracts.

(7) Desired military presence by US and HN chain of command. Military footprint may be reduced by leveraging contract support.

c. Identifying Military Capability Shortfalls that Require Contract Solutions.

(1) Determine mission essential services to be provided by contractors.

(2) Determine alternative means of support for mission essential services in the event a primary contractor is unable to perform.

d. Identification and Prioritization of Contracting Means and Organizational Structure.

(1) Conduct an initial "speed" vs. "quality" vs. "cost" assessment for essential services.

(2) Assess availability and suitability of standing CAP contracts. Conduct "speed, quality, cost" assessment for CAP vs. the availability of theater support contracts.

(3) Assess the availability of non-DOD contracts for required support (e.g., DOS, PN, and HNS contracts).

(4) Determining which of three contracting related organizational options will be most suitable for operation (e.g., Operational Contract Support Theater Support Contracting Command, Lead Service, or Service Component support to own forces).

4. CSIP Planning Considerations

Information from the completed mission analysis assists planners in preparing their CSIP. The below considerations are not comprehensive but may also serve as a guide in planning efforts. Planners can use the JOPES sample format for annex W of an OPLAN/CONPLAN as a template in structuring their respective portions of a plan.

5. General Questions

a. What is the main mission, level of forces deploying, location, duration, and type of contingency contracting required?

b. Are CAAF support requirements incorporated in the logistic requirements estimate?

c. Is there/will there be a lead Service designated for CUL?

d. Will single Service, lead Service, or joint organization execute the theater support contracting effort?

e. Are there trigger points to move from single Service to lead Service to a joint command (or from joint command to a lead Service organization)?

f. Are HCAs and associated SCOs properly identified to include primary duties, location, and flow of contracting authority?

g. What triggers would require movement of HCA within or out of operational area?

h. How will the organization be structured (by buying activity, geographical area, customer, etc.), to include flows of authority?

i. How many forces will the contracting organization support; how many contracting officers/administrators are needed?

j. Will there be stability operations related transition and reconstruction requirements? If so, are facilities reconstruction related requirements addressed? See JP 3-34, *Joint Engineer Operations,* for details on DOD construction agents.

k. Will contracting organization support other federal government or non-governmental agencies?

l. Did/will DOD designate an executive agent responsible for contracting?

m. Which Service will provide the majority of the contingency contracting officers?

n. What contracting support agencies will be needed, and what contracting relationship will they have with the deployed contracting unit?

o. How will the contracting organization and supply system interact to ensure no duplication of effort?

p. How will the contracting organization interface with financial management, legal, and supply?

q. Will external support logistical related contracts be utilized (i.e., LOGCAP, AFCAP, DLA prime vendor)? If so, how will these external support contracts be managed to ensure there is no undue competition for the limited commercial vendor base? In addition, is there a plan to reduce the reliance on expatriate US citizen employees in order to reduce the overall cost of external support service contracts?

r. Are specific contract administration delegations in place? Are ACO requirements, to include location and reporting chain, identified?

s. Are there reach-back arrangements made to non-deployed contracting and/or legal counsel organizations?

t. How will contract visibility be maintained?

u. What existing ACSAs and HNS agreements are in place? How will they impact contracting support?

v. What agency will perform the contract administration for external support/systems support/theater support contracting?

w. Are there plans, policies, and procedures along with sufficient theater support contracting capabilities in place to allow for CAP task orders to be routinely transferred over to theater support contracts?

x. What type of banking/financial institutions will be available?

y. What information concerning potential sources for contracted support is currently available (see US embassy, consulate attaches, DLA, etc.)?

z. Will the contracting organization use foreign funds?

aa. Who will establish procurement priorities?

ab. Will there be a JARB and/or JCSB established? If so, are the required contracting organization members of these boards identified to include the chairperson of the JCSB?

ac. Are the major requiring activities identified and advised of approximate administrative and procurement lead times for contracted support?

ad. Will there be extensive use of GPC or FOOs? What procedures are needed to manage and control these programs?

ae. Are there adequate CORs identified and trained to assist in managing contractor performance?

af. Is a civil-military operations center (CMOC) established or are civil affairs personnel available to provide market research information?

ag. Main operating and forward operating base CSIPs. Do they exist? Should they exist? If they exist, are they properly integrated into the GCC or subordinate JFC CSIP?

ah. Are there FAR relief procedures and guidance in-place (simplified acquisition threshold raised) and what relief will be considered necessary? Can this relief be pre-arranged?

ai. What is the funding source(s), and will financial management personnel deploy?

aj. Are there mechanisms for tax relief?

ak. Are operational specific policies and procedures, published in orders, and/or other policy documents available?

al. To what extent will contracting have to be utilized to provide support due to the absence of organic capability and/or to offset the impact of any force caps on the size of the military force?

am. What OGAs will be in the operational area, what will they be doing, and what will they be contracting for?

6. Local Vendor Base and Other Local Considerations

a. What supplies and services can be procured from the local populace?

b. Are there local customs, laws, taxes, or language barriers that will make contracting with the local vendors difficult?

c. What HNS, SOFAs, ACSAs, and other diplomatic/international/multinational agreements will be in effect?

d. What is the local currency, and how fluid/stable is the currency?

e. What payment mechanism will be required by vendors?

f. Will local vendors be capable of providing emergency response?

g. Will local vendors accept GPCs?

h. What cultural issues exist with business operations?

i. Are sources available for pre-identified requirements (are maps available showing location of vendors)?

j. How/where will vendors deliver commodities to the base?

k. How robust is the vendor base in the AOR?

l. Are there requirements that can't be procured locally; what are the workarounds?

m. What assistance will the US Embassy provide?

n. Who are my US Embassy Point of Contacts?

7. Logistical and Communications Questions

a. How reliable is the infrastructure (roads, sewer, electric, water)?

b. What security measures are required for intratheater travel? Are security personnel available for augmentation?

c. Are interpreter services required?

d. What computer/automation network capability will be available?

e. What communication capabilities will be available (internet, cell phones, Defense Switched Network, etc.)?

f. How will requiring activities and contracting organizations communicate with contracting units, requiring activities in the field, and with local vendors?

g. Will communication capabilities provide contracting personnel the necessary equipment for reach-back purchases?

h. Are deployable contingency contracting kits required?

i. What facilities, equipment, and other support will be needed; are appropriate items identified in the time-phased force and deployment data?

j. Will contracting personnel be required (allowed) to go off base? Will civilian clothing be required (authorized)?

k. What military airlift is available for the movement of supplies or personnel?

l. Are military convoy channels established? If not, will escorts be provided?

Intentionally Blank

APPENDIX F
CONTRACTOR MANAGEMENT PLANNING CONSIDERATIONS AND CHECKLIST

1. General

The following checklist is intended to be used as a guide for the GCC, subordinate JFC and Service component commanders and staffs to ensure that key contractor management requirements are addressed in all OPLANs/OPORDs. This checklist is intended to highlight key contractor management challenges, issues and areas of concern that routinely confront the JFC and subordinate Service component commands in military operations. Since contractor management responsibilities cross all primary and special staff lines of responsibility, this checklist is designed to assist the commander in establishing individual primary and special staff responsibilities for the different areas of contractor management planning. Since the CMP must be synchronized with the relevant content of the CSIP, it is imperative that contracting planners are involved when crafting the CMP.

2. Contractor Management Considerations

The questions below are intended to highlight key contractor management challenges, issues and areas of concern that routinely confront the JFC and subordinate Service component commands in military operations. Since contractor management responsibilities cross all primary and special staff lines of responsibility, these questions are designed to assist the commander in establishing individual primary and special staff responsibilities.

a. General Contractor Management Planning Questions.

(1) Are the GCC, subordinate JFC and Service component commanders and staffs aware of the general scope and scale of contracted support to be utilized for the operation? (J-4 contracting staff lead; all other staff elements assist)

(2) Have the GCC, subordinate JFC and Service component commanders assessed the overall contractor management requirement and provided specific guidance on how they will organize and execute contractor management planning? (J-5 lead; all other staff elements assist)

(3) Has a joint contractor management planning group been established? If so, which staff elements are required to participate? What is their battle rhythm? Which staff element has the lead for this effort? (J-5 lead; all other staff elements assist)

(4) Will a stand-alone CMP be developed within annex W or will the specific contractor management requirements be addressed in related sections of the OPLAN/OPORD? If a stand-alone CMP is to be developed, which staff office is responsible to lead this effort? (J-5 lead; all other staff elements assist)

(5) Are the GCC, subordinate JFC, and Service component staff members aware of basic contractor management policies, doctrine as found in the DODI 3020.41, *Contractor Personnel Authorized to Accompany the US Armed Forces*, CJCSM 3122.03B, *Joint Operation Planning and Execution System (JOPES) Volume II, Planning Formats*, this

publication and other associated policy and doctrine publications? (J-5 lead; all other staff elements assist)

(6) Are there existing GCC or Service contractor management policies? If so, are key staff members aware of these policies and how they affect contractor management planning in their functional areas? (No specific lead; all staff elements assist)

(7) Are the subordinate Service component commanders prepared to execute proper contractor management to include ensuring that there are adequate CORs identified and certified? (No specific lead; all staff elements assist)

(8) Are special contract oversight management units such as DCMA and the Army component's LOGCAP – forward- part of the deployment package? (J-3 lead; J-4 assist)

b. Contractor Personnel Legal Status and Discipline.

(1) Are the GCC, subordinate JFC, and Service component commanders and members of their legal staffs aware of contractor personnel legal status (including latest information on UCMJ applicability) and discipline authority over the different types of contractor employees per DOD policy and approved doctrine? (SJA lead)

(2) Are there AOR-wide and/or specific operational focused contractor personnel discipline policies in place? Do these policies include specific contractor personnel discipline procedures? (SJA lead)

(3) Have subordinate commanders been made aware of these specific contractor personnel discipline related policies and procedures? (SJA lead)

(4) Are there any current SOFA provisions and/or HN laws that restrict the employment of nonlocal national contractor personnel? (SJA lead)

c. Deployment/Redeployment Planning and Preparation

(1) Have specific theater entrance requirements been established for CAAF? (Supported GCC J-3 lead)

(2) Have CAAF and their associated equipment been added to the TPFDD? (J-5 lead; J-4 and J-3 assist)

(3) Have these requirements been published IAW CJCSM 3122.02C, *Joint Operation Planning and Execution System (JOPES) Volume III, Crisis Action Time-Phased Force and Deployment Data Development and Deployment Execution*, DFARS Sub-Part 225.74, *Defense Contracts Outside the United States*, and DFARS PGI 225.7401, *Contracts Requiring Performance or Delivery in a Foreign Country*? (J-3 lead; J-2 [intelligence directorate of a joint staff], J-4 contracting staff, SJA, surgeon assist)

(4) Have the service components completed their planning for the continuation of essential services IAW DODI 3020.37, *Continuation of Essential DOD Contractor Services During Crisis*? (J-5 lead; J-4 assist)

(5) Have steps been taken to mitigate the risks associated with the use of contracted support? (J-5 lead; J-4 assist)

(6) Have mission essential contracted support requirements been identified? (J-5 lead; J-4 assist)

(7) Does the contract clearly obligate contractors to continue essential contractor services during a contingency operation even in the event of hostile acts? (J-4 contracting staff)

(8) Are responsibilities assigned to ensure effective FP (to include PR) and security of CAAF as dictated by the local threat environment? (J-5 lead; J-2, J-3, J-4 contracting staff assist)

(9) Have plans been developed to replace CAAF who are performing essential contractor services in contingency operations or to otherwise mitigate the loss of services? This includes assessing alternative sources (military, DOD civilian, local, national, or other contractor(s)) or taking other actions that will mitigate the loss of such support. (J-5 lead; J-1 and J-4 contracting staff assist)

(10) Have steps been taken to ensure contractor personnel are treated fairly and not subject to trafficking in persons schemes? (contracting officers lead; J-4 contracting staff, DCMA. and unit CORs assist)

(11) Are contractor management policies and procedural requirements incorporated in the contract? (contracting officers)

(12) For prearranged contracted support are standard DFARS deployment clauses in the contract to ensure that contractor employees understand and are prepared to execute their contract in a contingency environment? (contracting officers)

(13) For contracts let for specific operations, are operational specific contract clauses included in the PWS and other terms and conditions of the contract? (contracting officers, DCMA ACOs)

(14) Is contingency contractor employee status identified up front in the contracting process? Contractor status will drive the authorizations and privileges the contractor employee may receive. (contracting officers, DCMA ACOs)

(15) Does the contracting officer have published theater entrance requirements from the supported GCC for contractor personnel hired outside of the operational area? (contracting officers)

(16) Have all CAAF received a DD Form 489 Geneva Conventions ID Card? (Service component personnel staff, contracting officers, CORs)

(17) Have all CAAF received a CAC prior to deployment to the operational area? (Service component personnel staff, contracting officers, CORs)

(18) Do expiration dates on the DD Form 489 and CAC correspond to the end date of the contract period of performance? (Service component personnel staff and Service contracting officers, CORs)

(19) Has the PCO, or designee, validated requirements for and availability of government support at the deployment center, JRC, and within the operational area? (Requiring activity staff, contracting officers, CORs, requiring activities)

(20) Do all CAAF have an LOA issued by the PCO or designee? (contracting officers, CORs)

(21) Has medical surveillance screening (as prescribed in DODD 6490.02E, *Comprehensive Health Surveillance*) for CAAF been completed? (Service component personnel staff, contracting officers, CORs)

(22) Has general medical evaluation and immunizations for all CAAF been completed IAW published specific medical related theater entrance requirements? (Service component personnel staff; contracting officers, CORs)

(23) Have operational specific security screening and badge issuance policies and procedures for CAAF and non-CAAF who require routine access to military facilities been published? (J-1 lead; J-3 assist)

(24) Does the contract contain DFARS clause 252.225-7040 paragraph (g) specifying use of the DOD designated contractor personnel management system of record as the database to establish and track accountability for deployed contractors? (contracting officer)

(25) Are CAAF properly entered into DOD designated contractor personnel management system of record prior to deployment? (Prime contractor; contracting officer/ACO)

(26) Do all CAAF have adequate protective clothing and equipment as specified in the contract? This includes any individual GFE items, IAW JFC directives and Service policies. (contracting officers, CORs)

(27) Do contractor personnel authorized to wear distinctive military uniforms have and carry written authorization? (contracting officers, CORs). If applicable, are the uniforms and protective equipment in compliance with supported GCC and subordinate JFC guidance? (contracting officers, CORs)

(28) Have CAAF completed all current DOD required standard training and any operational-specific supported GCC, subordinate JFC, and Service mandated training? (contracting officers, CORs)

(29) Have CAAF completed legal status familiarization to ensure they understand their legal status IAW international law to include prevention of human trafficking information? (contracting officers, CORs)

(30) Have CAAF completed familiarization training on US laws, HNS laws and SOFAs that contractor personnel may be subject to? (contracting officers, CORs)

(31) Have all CAAF completed basic law of war training and have selected CAAF completed advanced training commensurate with their duties and responsibilities, as necessary (e.g., security personnel and contract interrogators)? (contracting officers, CORs)

(32) Have CAAF completed law of war training related to the handling of EPWs and detainees (required for all CAAF who may come into to contact with detainees or EPWs)? (contracting officers, CORs)

(33) Have CAAF completed PR training and isolated personnel reports as determined by the requiring activity and supported JFC/Service component? (contracting officers, CORs)

(34) Have CAAF completed medical awareness training related to local health risks, medical related policies and procedures? (contracting officers, CORs)

(35) Have contractor personnel completed theater specific requirements (FP/security, hazard awareness, wear and use of protective gear, etc.) (required for all CAAF as directed by the supported GCC, subordinate JFC, and Service components; may include in-theater briefings to non-CAAF employees whose area performance is on a US base or in the immediate vicinity of US forces)? (contracting officers, CORs)

(36) Are CAAF being deployed into an operational area properly certified and fully integrated into the supported GCC and subordinate JFC's deployment plan IAW one of the contractor personnel certification and deployment methodologies? (Service component personnel and operations officer lead; Service contracting officers, CORs assist)

(a) Process and deploy with the supported unit. (supported unit personnel and operations officers; Service contracting officer)

(b) Process and deploy as a non-unit related personnel. (Service component personnel, operations officers and contracting officers)

(c) Self-certification and/or deployment. (Service component personnel, operations officers and contracting officers)

(37) Do CAAF meet the supported GCC and subordinate JFC prescribed training and preparation standards prior to entering the operational area? (Service component operations personnel and contracting officers)

(38) Are contract personnel being deployed into the operational area properly integrated into the time phased force and development process? (Service component operations officers and contracting officers)

(39) Are redeploying contractor personnel properly managed and controlled?

(a) Has the appropriate contractor personnel accountability database been updated? (contracting officer)

(b) Have government issued badges and ID cards been recovered? (prime contractor; contracting officer/ACO)

(c) Has all GFE or CAGO equipment been recovered? (contracting officer and COR)

(d) Has redeployment medical screening been completed (CAAF only)? (contracting officer and COR)

(e) Have all required debriefings been completed? (various Service component staff)

(f) Have security clearances been withdrawn as applicable? (contracting officer)

d. In-Theater Contractor Personnel Management

(1) Are all CAAF directed to be processed in and out of the operational area through a JRC or other personnel centers/processes designated by the JFC? (contracting officer)

(2) Has transportation been arranged for the contractor and their equipment to the point of performance? (J-3 lead; J-4 assist)

e. Force Protection

(1) Has the JFC and/or designated subordinate Service or designee developed operational specific procedures to provide security? (J-3)

(2) Are contractor personnel requiring access to military facilities incorporated in the overall FP and security plans? (J-3 lead; J-2, J-4 assist)

(3) Has the contracting officer included operational specific FP, security, and PR related information into the contract? (contracting officer)

(4) Does the contract specify all contingency contractor personnel whose area of performance is in the vicinity of US forces shall be required to comply with applicable supported GCC, subordinate JFC, and subordinate commanders' FP policies and procedures? (contracting officer)

(5) Have JFC and subordinate commanders developed local policies and procedures to vet and badge all contractor employees who need routine access to military facilities? (J-3 lead; J-2 and J-4 contracting staff assist)

(6) Are all CAAF provided protection during transit within the operational area commensurate to protection provided to DOD civilians? (J-3)

(7) Has the JFC, lead Service, or multinational organization responsible for land movement control authority established, published, and implemented operational specific contractor related convoy FP standards and procedures? (J-3 lead; J-4 assist)

(8) Are individual contractor personnel arming policies in place and enforced? (J-3)

(9) Do contractor personnel authorized to carry weapons for personal protection meet applicable US, HN, and international law; relevant SOFAs or other international agreements; DOD policy; JFC established guidance? (SJA lead; J-3, J-4 contracting staff, contracting officer, COR assist)

(10) Are DOD security services provided by contractors IAW applicable US, HN, international law, and relevant SOFAs? (SJA lead; J-3, J-4 contracting staff, contracting officer, COR assist)

(11) Have all contractor personnel authorized to be armed been fully briefed on the US and HN laws, SOFAs, and JFC policies regarding the circumstances in which they may use force? (contracting officer)

(12) Does the contract contain provisions informing the contractor of any known or potentially hazardous situations to include general stipulations limiting this support to non-offensive operations and government responsibilities to provide back-up security support? (contracting officer)

f. Government Support to Contractor Personnel

(1) Is logistics support provided to contractors IAW subordinate JFC policy and coordinated with the requiring activity or affected commander prior to the contractor's arrival at the point of performance? (J-4)

(2) Have government provided contractor support requirements been identified, forwarded and coordinated with the unit or location providing the support? (contracting officer, J-4)

(a) Have contractor requirements for living space been identified and made available? (contracting officer, J-4)

(b) Have overall contractor personnel BOS requirements been planned for and are they supportable? (J-4)

(c) Have contractor requirements for work space and power requirements been identified by the contracting officer or designated ACO and coordinated with the appropriate JFC or Service component staff engineer? (J-4 and/or engineer lead; contracting officer assist)

(3) Are CAAF generally provided the same standards of support and living arrangements as DOD civilian personnel of similar grade and responsibility level? (J-4 lead; contracting officer, COR assist)

(4) Are CAAF afforded reasonable accommodations IAW DOD and GCC established standards? (J-4 lead; contracting officer, COR assist)

(5) Are appropriate clauses included in the contract for all CAAF who are expected to perform their duties in field conditions? (contracting officer)

(6) Do contracts specify that, when possible, subsistence support provided to contractors is provided on a non-reimbursable basis? (contracting officer)

(7) Have joint force and Service component planners accounted for Government provided support cost to contractors and contractor personnel? (J-4)

(8) Is the JFC prepared to provide emergency medical care to all contract employees, including CAAF employees who are injured in the immediate vicinity of US forces or on a US base? (joint force surgeon)

(9) Are the JFC and its Service components prepared to provide primary/routine medical care to CAAF as outlined by contractual requirements and as the mission dictates? (joint force surgeon lead; Service component and contracting staff and assist)

(10) Is the JFC prepared to record all costs associated with the treatment and transportation of contractor personnel to the selected civilian facility? (joint staff surgeon lead; Service component surgeon assist)

(11) If transfer of GFE and/or CAGO equipment is anticipated, has the JFC's J-4 properly coordinated disposition instructions with the appropriate DOS, DOD, and affected

component organization to ensure that the instructions are clearly understood and provided in a timely manner? (J-4; Service component contracting staff assist)

(12) If authorized, are contractor postal support requirements provided? (J-1)

(13) Is the specific nature and extent of mortuary affairs support determined and communicated to military forces and contractors through governing OPLANs/OPORDs and contractual documents? (J-4)

(14) Are authorizations for CAAF use of military exchange facilities for health and comfort items coordinated and identified in the individual terms and conditions in the contract? (J-4 lead; contracting officers assist)

(15) Are CAAF allowed access to deployed MWR facilities or programs? Is this access coordinated and identified in the individual terms and conditions in the contract? (Contracting Officer and CORs lead; J-1 assist)

g. Coordinating Non-DOD Contract Support

(1) Is the JFC prepared to assist to integrate non-DOD contractor personnel and equipment into both air and surface movements as required? (J-3 lead; J-4 assist)

(2) Does the subordinate JFC have a requirement to provide back-up security support to DOS or other non-DOD organizations? If so, are these organizations using private security firms for protection? (J-3)

(a) What is the subordinate JFC's authority, if any, in planning and utilizing non-DOD contracted security firms? (J-3)

(b) Where are these security firms operating? (J-3)

(c) What is their RUF? Did the JFC have input to the RUF? (J-3)

(d) Has the JFC, COM and other interested parties developed workable and reliable information sharing, communication mechanisms? (J-3 lead; J-6 assist)

(e) Are subordinate commanders properly informed of and prepared to execute back-up security requirements? (J-3 lead; Service component operations staff assist)

(f) Have the subordinate commanders conducted proper coordination with security firms and/or rehearsed back-up security actions? (J-3 lead; Service component operations staff assist).

Intentionally Blank

APPENDIX G
NOTIONAL LEAD SERVICE AND JOINT THEATER SUPPORT CONTRACTING COMMAND ORGANIZATIONS

1. General

There is no formally approved, established model for the lead Service theater support or joint theater support contracting command organizational option. In general, the lead Service option should be considered for major, long-term operations where two or more Service components having significant forces operating within the same operational area. The joint theater support contracting command organizational option is normally only applicable for major, long-term, complex stability operations where the subordinate JFC needs direct control over all aspects of theater support contracting. Normally, the lead Service theater support contracting organization will be derived from either an Air Force expeditionary contracting squadron or an Army CSB. Likewise, these same two organizations would normally form the core of a joint theater support contracting command. Figure G-1 depicts a notional lead Service theater support contracting organization and Figure G-2 depicts a typical joint theater support contracting command organization. This appendix describes only one manner to organize these contracting commands. The actual organization structure of the lead Service contracting command or joint theater support contracting command will be based on operational factors such as the base organization structure, mission requirements, major customer orientation, commercial support base, etc. For example, the joint theater support contracting command may be organized along support function lines (e.g., transportation, medical, infrastructure) rather than the forces support, HN forces/transition, and reconstruction support model depicted in Figure G-2.

2. Lead Service Staff and Subordinate Organization Overview

a. **Commander.** The commander of a lead Service theater support contracting organization would normally be an O-6 with significant contingency contracting experience. This commander typically reports through Service channels to the Service component commander, but has overall responsibility to ensure that the theater support contracting mission within the JFC designated operational area is conducted in an effective, efficient, and well coordinated fashion.

b. **Deputy.** Like all chiefs of staff, the joint theater contracting command chief of staff is responsible to integrate all special and primary staff functions within the command. Normally, this position would be an O-6 with contingency contracting experience.

c. **Administrative Staff.** The commander's administrative staff is normally sourced from the lead Service. This support requires no specific rank or any contracting related experience.

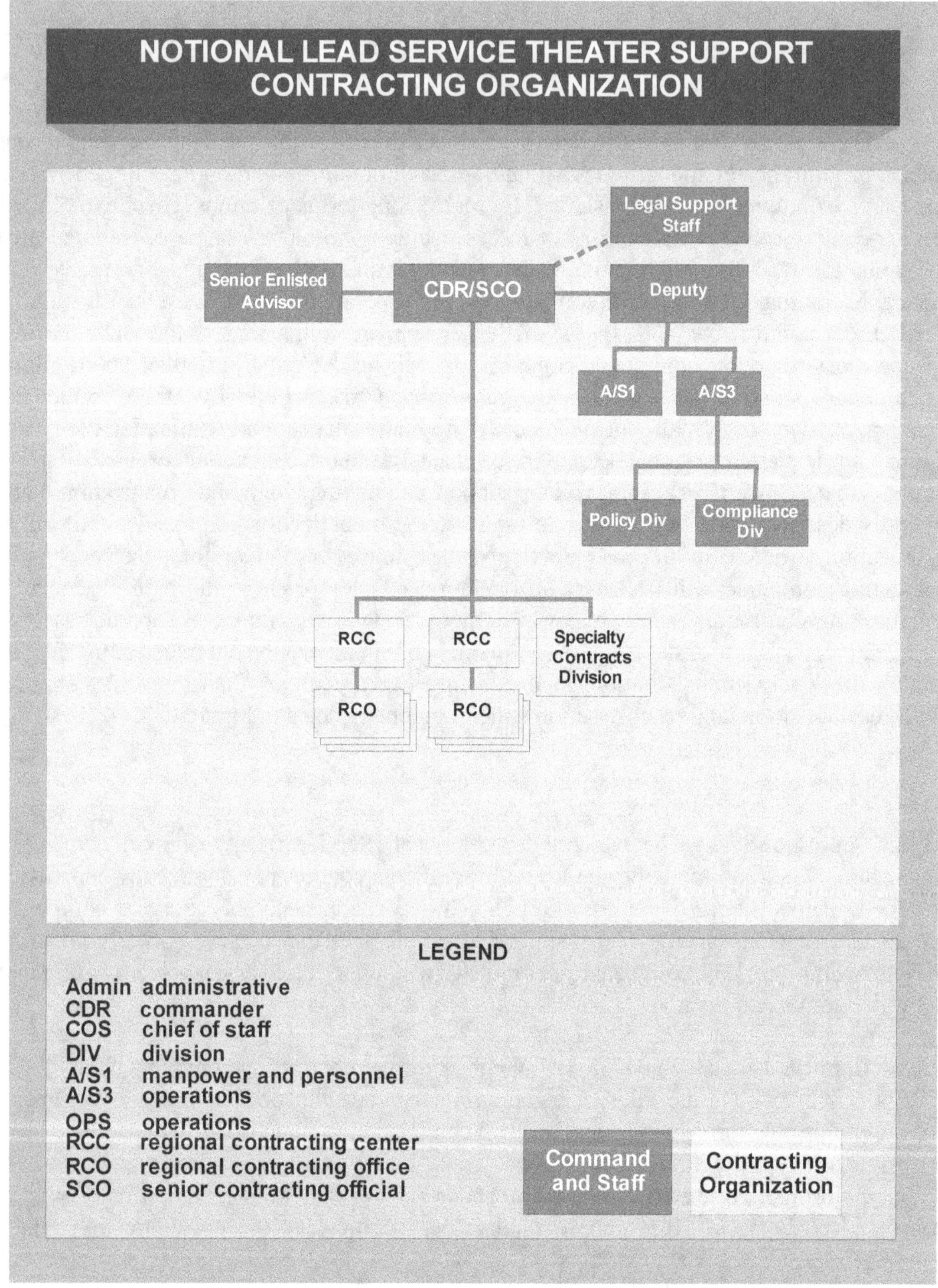

Figure G-1. Notional Lead Service Theater Support Contracting Organization

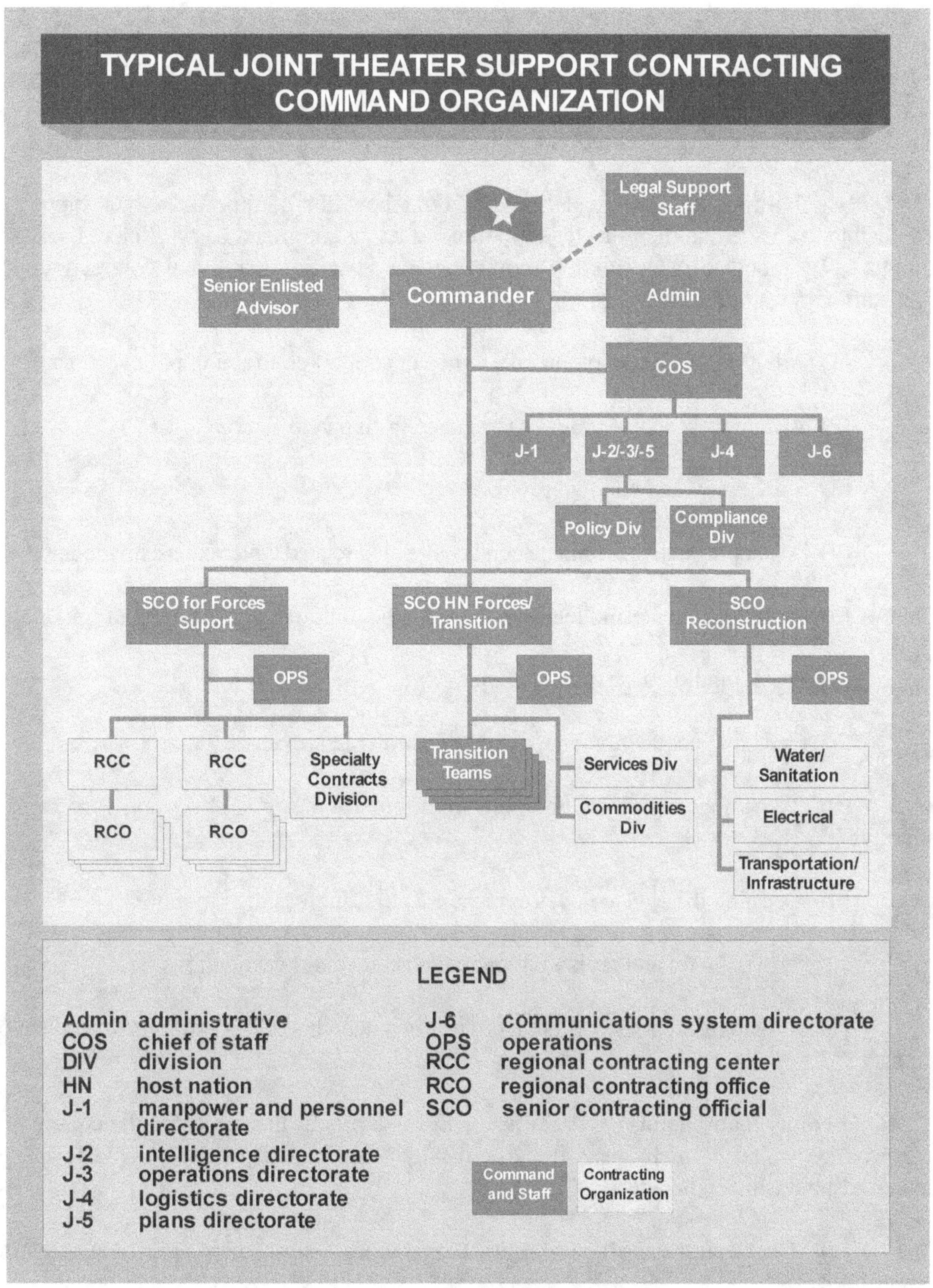

Figure G-2. Typical Joint Theater Support Contracting Command Organization

d. **Primary Staff.** As with the commander's administrative staff, the lead Service theater support contracting organization will normally retain the organic staff arrangements of the Service contracting organization responsible to execute this mission. In most cases, some augmentation may be required in two specific primary staff functions. These functions are; plans and operations, and policy and compliance.

e. **Legal Support.** The lead Service component for common contract support is responsible to ensure that their theater support contracting command has sufficient fiscal and contract law support to meet mission requirements. Specific operational contract support legal staff responsibilities include:

(1) Advising on the development of theater support contracting policy.

(2) Arranging reach-back legal assistance from parent Service.

(3) Solicitation and contract review.

(4) Developing and providing general contracting related ethics counseling/training.

(5) Providing advice and legal reviews related to potential procurement fraud.

(6) Providing litigation management.

(7) Providing acquisition and source selection plan reviews.

(8) Providing advice on Freedom of Information Act (FOIA) and Privacy Act requests.

(9) Assisting the JFC to develop responses to Congressional inquiries.

(10) Advising on and reviewing command-directed investigations.

(11) Providing advice/reviews on protests and unauthorized commitments/ratification actions.

f. **Senior Contracting Official(s).** Lead Service theater support contracting organizations would normally have the commander "dual hatted" as the SCO. The SCO's general responsibilities include:

(1) Overseeing day-to-day contract operations within their area of contracting responsibility.

(2) Overseeing and assessing the effectiveness of their contracting programs.

(3) Issuing warrants; determining delegated warrant authorities for assigned and attached contracting officers.

(4) Directing subordinates to participate in the JARB (normally advisory capacity only).

(5) Chairing the JCSB as directed.

(6) Directing procurement management reviews or contract management reviews.

(7) Developing and providing management control oversight.

(8) Conducting special reviews as required.

(9) Managing contract audit programs.

(10) Managing suspension debarment programs.

g. **Regional Contracting Center(s) (RCC).** RCCs are normally led by a warranted O-5 and may be augmented with other Service contracting personnel. RCCs' specific make-up depends on the specific mission support requirement, but could consist of between 10-25 warranted contracting officers, enlisted members, and/or DOD civilians. Aligning RCCs to major land force (i.e., division, corps, Marine expeditionary force) HQ or Air Force wings or groups is also common practice. **Key to the proper manning of these RCCs and their subordinate regional contracting offices (RCOs) is not the rank of the contracting officers on staff, but the warrant and experience level of the staff.**

h. **Regional Contracting Office(s).** RCOs are contracting organizations under the C2 of the head of an RCC. An RCO could be jointly staffed or staffed entirely with lead Service personnel. RCOs are normally led by an O-4 contracting officer and are made up of anywhere from 2-8 warranted contracting officers, enlisted members, and/or DOD civilians. The actual size and make-up of an RCO is based on actual mission support requirements. RCOs normally provide area support to specific forward operating bases and/or designated areas within the JOA.

i. **Specialty Contracts Division.** In some operations, there may be a need to develop a specialty contracts division that can provide contracting support for common, JOA-wide services or supplies. Additionally, these contracting organizations may also be utilized to perform complex contracting actions that exceed the RCC and RCO capabilities. The specialty contracts division will be made up of specially selected, highly trained contracting officers, NCOs, and/or DOD civilians who have the requisite experience and warrant to handle large, complex contract actions.

3. Joint Theater Support Contracting Command Staff and Subordinate Organization Overview

a. **Commander.** The commander of a joint theater support contracting command would normally be an O-7 or O-8 with significant contingency contracting experience. Due to the manner the Services develop their contingency contracting officers this will normally be an Air Force, Navy, or Army general/flag officer. The joint theater support contracting command commander reports to the subordinate JFC and has overall responsibility to ensure that the theater support contracting mission is conducted in an effective, efficient, and well coordinated fashion. This commander would also serve as the subordinate JFC's principal operational contract support advisor.

b. **Administrative Staff.** The commander's administrative staff support is determined by the joint theater support contracting command commander. This support requires no specific rank or any contracting related experience.

c. **Chief of Staff.** Like all chiefs of staff, the joint theater support contracting command chief of staff is responsible to integrate all special and primary staff functions within the command. Normally, this position would be an O-6 with contingency contracting experience.

d. **J-1.** The joint theater support contracting command J-1 performs normal joint personnel support to include working personnel assignments, JMD related actions, awards and ratings, etc. The J-1 normally would be a personnel officer with no specific rank or contracting related experience.

e. **J-2/3/5.** A joint theater support contracting command would not normally need a separate J-2 or J-5 office. The J-2/3/5 officer, normally an O-5 with contracting experience, has overall responsibility to assist the commander and SCO(s) to synchronize support to on-going and planned future operations. The J-2/3/5 focus is on supporting the subordinate JFC's intent with effective and efficient contracting actions. If needed, the J-2/3/5 could also contain separate policy and contract compliance divisions. Specific J-2/3/5 responsibilities would normally include:

(1) Monitoring subordinate JFC and subordinate organization operations.

(2) Assisting the commander in managing subordinate organization operations.

(3) Providing liaison to subordinate JFC's J-4 staff.

(4) Providing feedback on subordinate JFC operations, change to missions and priorities, etc.

(5) Reviewing daily JARB submission for contracting documents and PWS validation.

(6) Recommending changes to priorities of contracting effort to include movement of contracting officer resources between subordinate organizations.

(7) Recommending changes to JMD and staffing reflecting most effective operation of subordinate organizations.

(8) Developing, receiving and consolidating operational reports.

(9) Leading all policy related actions ICW the appropriate subordinate JFC staff and joint theater support contracting command subordinate organizations.

(10) Leading short-term and long-range planning actions.

(11) Developing and implementing command training programs.

(12) Establishing, collecting, and analyzing measures of effectiveness on civil impacts of contracting actions.

(13) Ensuring the command is in compliance with the FAR and DFARS.

(14) Establishing and implementing contracting policy for all subordinate contracting activities.

(15) Responding to FOIA and other inquiries.

(16) Processing unauthorized commitment, unsolicited proposals, and protest override actions.

(17) Coordinating and resolving contracting officer qualification and warrant issues.

(18) Coordinating joint theater support contracting command participation in/leadership of the CLPSB, JARB and JCSB as directed by the subordinate JFC.

f. **J-4.** The joint theater support contracting command J-4 would perform normal joint logistic actions to include general office supply actions, coordinating facility support, etc. The J-4 normally would be a logistics officer with no specific rank or contracting related experience requirements.

g. **J-6.** The joint theater support contracting command J-6 would perform normal joint communications support related actions to include coordinating communications support, website management, etc. The J-6 normally would be a communications/signal officer with no specific rank or contracting related experience.

h. **Legal Support.** The JFC legal staff is responsible to support the JFC and joint theater support contracting command in fiscal and contract law support matters. The JFC legal staff also establishes and implements JFC's acquisition legal policy. Other operational contract support related legal staff support include:

(1) Providing solicitation and contract review.

(2) Developing and providing general contract related ethics counseling/training.

(3) Providing advice and legal reviews related to potential procurement fraud.

(4) Providing litigation management.

(5) Providing acquisition and source selection plan reviews.

(6) Providing advice on FOIA and Privacy Act requests.

(7) Assisting the J2/3/5 to develop responses to Congressional inquiries.

i. **Senior Contracting Officer(s).** Joint theater contracting commands would normally have one to three SCOs, normally at the O-6 (or DOD civilian equivalent) level with significant contract related experience and certifications. The SCO's general responsibilities include:

(1) Overseeing day-to-day contract operations within their area of contracting responsibility.

(2) Overseeing and assessing the effectiveness of their contracting programs.

(3) Issuing warrants, determining delegated warrant authorities.

(4) Participating in the JARB (primarily the SCO Forces Support).

(5) Chairing the JCSB as directed.

(6) Managing and execute Procurement Management Reviews.

(7) Developing and providing oversight their Management Control Programs.

(8) Conducting special reviews as required.

(9) Managing Contract Audit Follow-up Program.

(10) Managing suspension and/or debarment actions.

j. **Senior Contracting Official Operations Staff.** Each SCO will normally have an operations staff with primary duties that mirror the joint theater support contracting command J-staff functions listed above. These staffs can vary in size and should be made up of officers and NCOs with at least some contracting/acquisition experience.

k. **Senior Contracting Official for Forces Support.** The SCO forces support is overall responsible to plan, coordinate, and manage theater support contracting for deployed US forces and multinational forces support. This support may also include support to interagency personnel and facilities, but does not normally include support to OGA-led civil reconstruction projects. SCO forces support will normally have three or more RCCs each with multiple RCOs. SCO forces support may have a specialty contracting division to handle common, JOA-wide, and/or complex contracts that exceed RCC and RCO capabilities.

(1) **Regional Contracting Centers.** RCCs are joint staffed contracting organizations that are normally led by a warranted O-5. RCCs' specific makeup is depends on the specific mission support requirement but could consist of between 10-25 warranted contracting officers, NCOs, and/or DOD civilians. Aligning RCCs to major land force HQ (i.e., division, corps, Marine expeditionary force) or Air Force wings or groups is also common practice. **Key to the proper manning of these RCCs and their subordinate RCOs is not the rank of the contracting officers on staff, but the warrant and experience level of the staff.**

(2) **Regional Contracting Offices.** RCOs are joint staffed contracting organizations under the C2 of the lead of an RCC. RCOs are normally led by an O-4 contracting officer and are made up of anywhere from 2-8 warranted contracting officers, enlisted members, and/or DOD civilians. The actual size and make-up of an RCO is based on actual mission support requirements. RCOs normally provide area support to specific forward operating bases and/or designated areas within the JOA.

(3) **Specialty Contracts Division.** In some operations, there may be a need to develop a specialty contracts division that can provide contracting support for common, JOA-wide services or supplies. Additionally, this division may also be utilized to perform complex contracting actions that exceed the RCC and RCO capabilities. The specialty contracts division will be made up of specially selected, highly trained contracting officers, NCOs, and/or DOD civilians who have the requisite experience and warrant to handle large, complex contract actions.

l. **Senior Contracting Official for Host Nation Forces and Transition Support.** This SCO for HN and transition support is overall responsible to plan, coordinate, and manage theater support contracting actions in support of the subordinate JFC mission t in regards to HN security forces. The SCO for HN and transition support is also responsible to provide training and transition assistance to HN security forces (and other governmental agencies as directed) in developing and sustaining their own contracting support capabilities. SCO HN and transition support will normally include multiple transition teams and support divisions.

(1) **Service and Commodity Divisions.** The SCO for HN forces and transition support would normally have some type of subordinate contracting organization (or organizations) responsible to manage HN security forces theater support contracting actions that cannot be readily accommodated by the existing SCO forces support, RCCs, and/or RCOs. One way to organize to meet this requirement is stand-up separate services and commodities divisions. Another approach is to establish divisions based upon customer support. For example, a mission support division consisting of notionally J-4 and J-7 and an infrastructure support division made up of notionally J-6, engineering, and medical customers. These organizations would vary in size and would be staffed with warranted contracting officers, enlisted members, and/or DOD civilians. No specialized contracting experience would be required for these personnel.

(2) **Transition Teams.** If established, the SCO for HN and transition support will normally have multiple transition teams. These transition teams are responsible to plan and execute support to the development of HN security force and, if directed, HN governmental contracting support organizations and capabilities. These teams will vary in size, but must be manned with military or DOD civilian personnel with the requisite contracting experience required by their assigned mission. For example, a HN governmental transition support team would need to be staffed with military members and/or DOD civilian with significant and high-level contracting experience.

m. **Senior Contracting Official for Reconstruction Support.** The SCO reconstruction has overall responsibility to plan, coordinate, and manage theater support contracting actions in support of civil reconstruction. Normally, the SCO reconstruction would be in direct support of the US COM and/or the United States Agency for International Development. The SCO reconstruction would normally have multiple sector support contracting organizations. These subordinate organizations could include, but are not limited to, the following reconstruction sector areas: water, sanitation, electricity, transportation, oil production, etc. As much as resources permit, these staffs will be made up of specially selected, highly trained contracting officers, NCOs, and/or DOD civilians who have the requisite experience and warrant to handle large, complex reconstruction related contract actions.

APPENDIX H
REQUIREMENTS DEVELOPMENT AND ACQUISITION REVIEW PROCESSES

1. General

Prior to submitting any requirement to the contracting office, the requiring activity is responsible for creating a clear description of the requirement, performing market research, ensuring appropriate approvals are received, ensuring adequate funding is available, and ensuring procedures and points of contract for receipt of goods and services are established. Contracting offices typically do not perform contracting support without requiring activities first completing the aforementioned steps. The contracting office can not purchase any service, commodity, or construction prior to the completion of these requirements.

2. Clear Requirements Definition

a. **General.** One of the most important duties of the requiring activity is the proper description of the requirement. All future acquisition steps will flow from and are dependent on the proper description of the required item/service. The customer must be able to describe the minimum acceptable standard for the government. **Defining the minimal acceptable standard is crucial** to ensure proper utilization of limited government funds. **Often, the GCC and/or subordinate JFC staff will need to be directly involved in establishing and enforcing these standards.**

b. **Be as specific as possible.** A detailed description of the requirement is instrumental in allowing the contracting office to create a solicitation and the vendor to provide the right item/service. Without specificity in the requirements generation phase, the vendor may very well deliver a product or service that complies with the terms of the contract but doesn't meet the needs of the customer. For instance, stating you want "two dozen vehicle-mounted convoy warning signs written in the local language" inadequately conveys the desired attributes of the requirement. The customer must fully define the requirement. In this example, the requiring activity should identify the sign's required size, color, composition, the lettering script, size and color, weather durability, mounting capability, requested delivery dates, etc. The requiring activity should spell-out these attributes in its requirements documentation. Also, **the requiring activity, not the contracting officer, must ensure these requirements follow established JFC standards of support and other established guidance such as FP requirements.**

c. **Seek assistance early on.** Although the requiring activity must clearly define requirement, the contracting office and/or other special staff such as the subordinate JFC or Service component engineer staff, can provide useful advice early in the requirements definition process. Since the contracting office and other technical staff offices have probably seen similar requirements and solicitations, they probably have a good idea of some of the questions vendors may ask and/or can provide examples of PWS and/or IGE documents.

3. Market Research

a. **General.** Properly performed market research will greatly help the requiring activity define the requirement. While sometimes very challenging due to the local operational environment, the requiring activity must complete basic research to ensure required support is not already available through organic military support, multinational, and/or HNS sources. The requiring activity must also verify commercial availability of the required support. This commercial research includes determination of any commercial standards for the item of support along with potential local sources of support.

b. **Research Methodology**. While not available to all requiring activities in all operations, the internet is probably the single most valuable tool for performing market research. The requiring activity can use the internet to locate vendors, download item specifications, check warranty information, and determine delivery times. The requiring activity can also use the internet to download examples of the required items. It should be noted however, that submitting a brand-name in lieu of a detailed item description is generally not an approved acquisition strategy. The requirement should be couched in terms of defining characteristics that fulfill the need, not simply listing a specific brand/manufacturer.

c. **Do not obligate the Government.** Another commonly used approach to garner market research data is to call or visit vendors directly. Although this is an appropriate technique, care must be taken to ensure the vendor knows that the requiring activity is not placing an order or making a promise for future business.

4. Gaining Appropriate Approvals

a. **General.** An essential and often missed step in the requirements development process is ensuring the appropriate **functional staffs coordinate on the requirements package before it goes to contracting.** Depending on the requirement and local guidance, legal personnel may need to review it prior to submission to the commander for approval. Supply personnel may need to review requirements to verify the items are not available in the supply system. Communications personnel will need to ensure all communications and general automation requirements meet the standards and acquisition strategy set by the combatant command J-6 or equivalent. Medical personnel will review all requirements that may be associated with hazardous material. Also, construction projects will need to go through several review thresholds within the general engineering staff prior to submission to contracting. The local contracting unit can give requirements personnel additional guidance with regard to which offices/personnel need to review specific requirements.

b. Each requirement will also require **prioritization from the commanders in the field.** Depending on the requirement and the source of funding, each request for purchase will need to be approved and prioritized by the appropriate commander. Should the requirement be a joint controlled support item/service, the originating Service component organization will hold a service-unique requirements board (Acquisition Review Board) to validate and prioritize the Service's requests. Once approved by the Service process, the requirement will be sent to the JARB as depicted in Figure H-1.

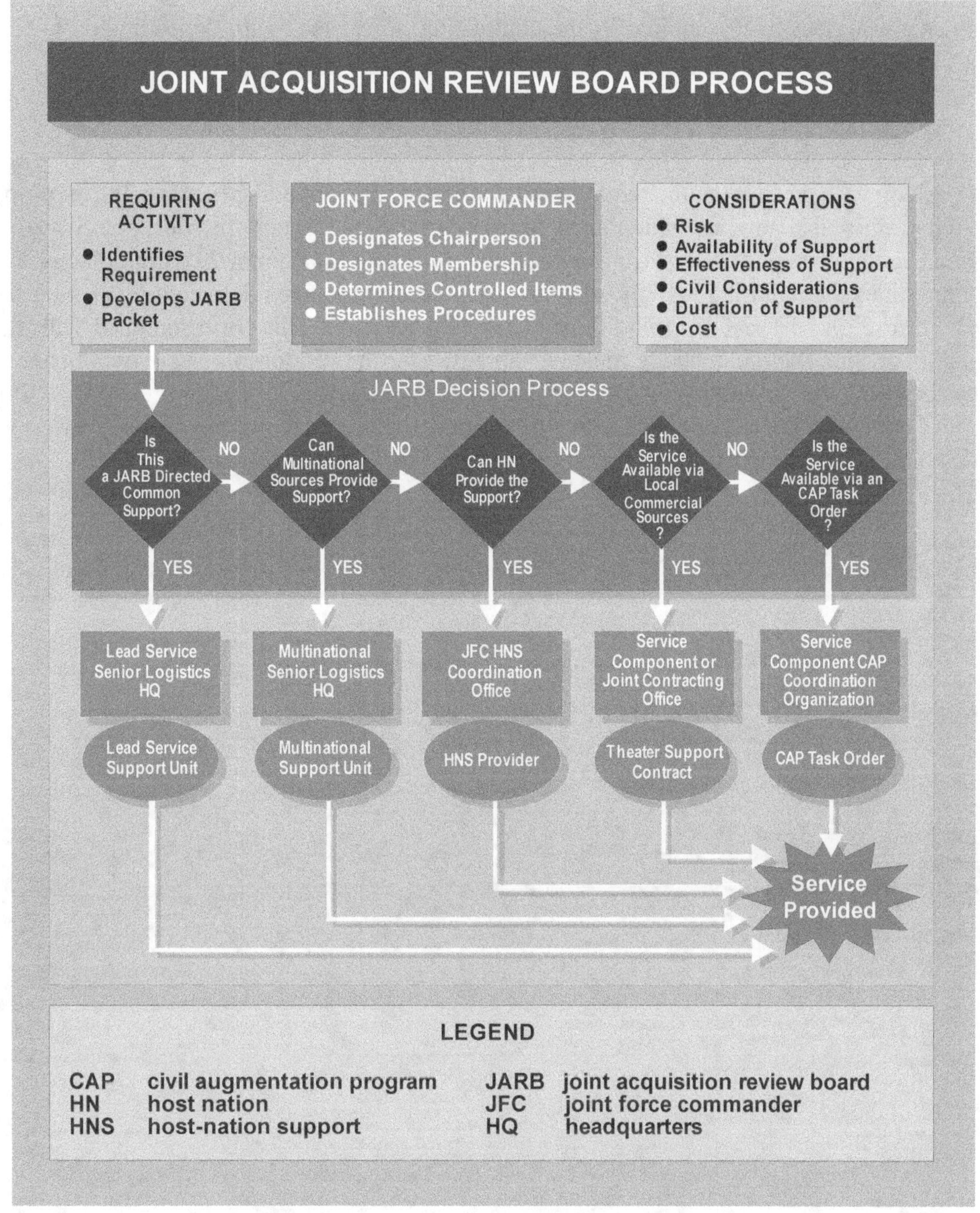

Figure H-1. Joint Acquisition Review Board Process

5. Receiving Funding

Although the requiring activity should have gone through some formal requirements definition process prior to the receipt of funding, the certified funding document is generally the start of the procurement process with the contracting office. The contracting office can not obligate the government with a contractual document prior to the receipt of funds. The acquisition timeline for the contracting office starts with a complete package which has a minimum consists of a valid requirements document(s) and a certified funding document (the extent of documents required by the contracting officer may vary depending on factors such as scope of effort, total dollar amount and complexity of the acquisition).

6. Receipt of Goods and Services

Along with developing the requirement documents and obtaining funding, the requiring activity must also provide individuals to receive the goods and provide some quality assurance that the goods or service provided complies with the contract's requirements. For commodities the requiring activity personnel will accept the items delivered by signing the DD Form 250, Material Inspection and Receiving Report. This form, coupled with the vendors invoice and the contract, must be submitted for the vendor to be paid by a financial management unit disbursing officer, or Defense Finance and Accounting Service. For service contracts, the requiring activity will normally be required to provide COR personnel to monitor contractor performance.

APPENDIX J
REFERENCES

The development of the JP 4-10 is based upon the following primary references:

1. International Law

a. Geneva Convention Relative to the Treatment of Prisoners of War.

b. Hague Convention of 1907.

2. US Government Publications

a. The Goldwater-Nichols Department of Defense Reorganization Act of 1986 (Title 10 USC Section Public Law 99-423).

b. *The National Security Strategy of the United States of America.*

c. *National Defense Strategy of the United States of America.*

d. *National Military Strategy.*

e. Title 10, United States Code.

f. Title 18, United States Code.

g. Title 38, United States Code.

h. Federal Acquisition Regulation (Title 48, CFR).

i. Deputy Secretary of Defense Memorandum, 25 September 2007, *Management of Contractor Personnel Accompanying US Armed Forces in Contingency Operations Outside the United States.*

j. Secretary of Defense Memorandum, 10 March 2008, *UCMJ Jurisdiction Over DOD Civilian Employees, DOD Contractor Personnel and Other Persons Serving with or Accompanying the Armed Forces Overseas During Declared War and in Contingency Operations.*

k. Deputy Secretary of Defense Memorandum, 24 Sep 07, *Policy Guidance for Provision of Medical Care to Department of Defense Civilian Employees Injured or Wounded While Forward Deployed in Support of Hostilities.*

3. DOD Publications

a. 2006 Quadrennial Defense Review.

b. Defense Federal Acquisition Regulation Supplement (DFARS), (Title 48, CFR, sections 201-299).

c. DOD 4515.13-R, *Air Transportation Eligibility.*

d. DOD 4525.6-M, *Department of Defense Postal Manual.*

e. DODD 1000.20, *Active Duty Service Determinations for Civilian or Contractual Groups.*

f. DODD 1100.4, *Guidance for Manpower Management.*

g. DODD 1300.22, *Mortuary Affairs Policy.*

h. DODD 2000.12, *DOD Antiterrorism (AT) Program.*

i. DODD 2310.2, *Personnel Recovery.*

j. DODD 2310.7, *Personnel Accounting – Losses Due to Hostile Acts.*

k. DODD 2311.01E DOD *Law of War Program.*

l. DODD 3000.05, *Military Support for Stability, Security, Transition, and Reconstruction Operations.*

m. DODD 5000.1, *The Defense Acquisition System.*

n. DODD 6200.3, *Emergency Health Powers on Military Installations.*

o. DODD 6490.02E, *Comprehensive Health Surveillance.*

p. DODI 6490.03, *Deployment Health.*

q. DODI 1000.1, *Identity Cards Required by the Geneva Convention.*

r. DODI 1000.13, *Identification (ID) Cards for Members of the Uniformed Services, Their Dependents, and Other Eligible Individuals.*

s. DODI 1100.19, *Wartime Manpower Mobilization Planning Policies and Procedures.*

t. DODI 1100.22, *Guidance for Determining Workforce Mix.*

u. DODI 1300.23, *Isolated Personnel Training for DOD Civilian and Contractors.*

v. DODI 1330.21, *Armed Services Exchange Regulations (ASER*).

w. DODI 2000.16, *DOD Antiterrorism (AT) Standards.*

x. DODI 3020.37, *Continuation of Essential DOD Contractor Services During Crises.*

y. DODI 3020.41, *Contractor Personnel Authorized to Accompany the US Armed Forces.*

z. DODI 4161.2, *Management, Control, and Disposal of Government Property in the Possession of Contractors.*

aa. DODI 5525.11, *Criminal Jurisdiction Over Civilians Employed By or Accompanying the Armed Forces Outside the United States, Certain Service Members, and Former Service Members.*

ab. DODI 6205.4, *Immunization of Other Than US Forces (OTUSF) for Biological Warfare Defense.*

ac. DODI 6490.03, *Deployment Health.*

ad. DOD O-2000.12H DOD *Antiterrorism (AT) Handbook.*

4. CJCS Publications

a. JP 1, *Doctrine for the Armed Forces of the United States.*

b. JP 1-0, *Personnel Support to Joint Operations.*

c. JP 1-02, *DOD Dictionary of Military and Associated Terms.*

d. JP 3-0, *Joint Operations.*

e. JP 3-07, *Antiterrorism.*

f. JP 3-10, *Joint Security Operations in the Theater.*

g. JP 3-33, *Joint Task Force Headquarters.*

h. JP 3-35, *Deployment and Redeployment Operations.*

i. JP 3-50, *Personnel Recovery.*

j. JP 4-0, *Joint Logistics.*

k. JP 4-06, *Mortuary Affairs in Joint Operations.*

l. CJCS Instruction 3141.01C, *Responsibilities for the Management and Review of Contingency Plans.*

m. CJCS Instruction 3270.01A, *Personnel Recovery within the Department of Defense* (U).

n. CJCSM 3122.02C, *Joint Operation Planning and Execution System (JOPES), Volume III, (Crisis Action Time-Phased Force, and Deployment Data Development, and Deployment Execution).*

o. CJCSM 3150.13B, *Joint Reporting Structure – Personnel Manual.*

5. Multi-Service Publications

a. Air Force Instruction 36-3026(I); Army Regulation 600-8-14; US Navy BUPERS Instruction 1750.10B; Marine Corps Order P5512.11C; Commandant Instruction M5512.1; Commissioned Corps Personnel Manual 29.2, Instructions 1 and 2; NOAA Corps Regulations, Chapter 1, Part 4, *Identification Cards for Members of the Uniformed Services, Their Eligible Family Members, and Other Eligible Personnel.*

b. Multi-Service Publication FM 4-01.45/ Marine Corps Reference Publication 4-11.3H/ US Navy Tactics, Techniques and Procedures 4-01.3/US Air Force Tactics, Techniques and Procedures (I) 3-2.58, *Multi-Service Tactics, Techniques and Procedures for Tactical Convoy Operations.*

6. Air Force Publications

a. Air Force FAR Supplement Appendix CC (Title 48, CFR, sections 5100-5199).

b. Air Force Materiel Command Fact Book.

7. Army Publications

a. Army FAR Supplement, (Title 48, CFR, Sections 5100-5199).

b. Army FAR Manual Number 2 (Contingency Contracting).

c. Army Corps of Engineers FAR Supplement.

d. FM 3-100.21, *Contractors on the Battlefield.*

e. FM 100-10-2, *Contracting Support on the Battlefield.*

f. FM-Interim 4-93.41, *Army Field Support Brigade Tactics, Techniques and Procedures.*

g. AR 715-9, *Army Contractors Accompanying the Force.*

h. AR 700–137, *Logistics Civil Augmentation Program (LOGCAP).*

i. US Army Training Support Packet (TSP) 151-M-001, *Contractors Accompanying the Force.*

8. Navy Publications

a. Navy Supply Systems Command Instruction 4230.37A.

b. Navy Supply Systems Command Instruction 713.

c. Secretary of the Navy Instruction 5400.15B, *Department of the Navy Research, Development and Acquisition, and Associated Life-Cycle Management Responsibilities.*

9. Marine Corps Publication

Marine Corps Order P4200.15, Appendix B.

10. Special Operations Command Publication

USSOCOM FAR Supplement (Title 48, CFR, sections 5100-5199).

11. DCMA Publication

DCMA Guidebook (CCAS Chapter).

Intentionally Blank

APPENDIX K
ADMINISTRATIVE INSTRUCTIONS

1. User Comments

Users in the field are highly encouraged to submit comments on this publication to: Commander, United States Joint Forces Command, Joint Warfighting Center, ATTN: Doctrine Group, 116 Lake View Parkway, Suffolk, VA 23435-2697. These comments should address content (accuracy, usefulness, consistency, and organization), writing, and appearance.

2. Authorship

The lead agent for this publication is the United States Army. The Joint Staff doctrine sponsor for this publication is the Director for Logistics (J-4).

3. Change Recommendations

a. Recommendations for urgent changes to this publication should be submitted:

TO: ALT-FO FORT LEE VA//ATCL-ALT-FO
INFO: JOINT STAFF WASHINGTON DC//J4/J7-JEDD//
CDRUSJFCOM SUFFOLK VA//DOC GP//

Routine changes should be submitted electronically to Commander, Joint Warfighting Center, Doctrine and Education Group and info the Lead Agent and the Director for Operational Plans and Joint Force Development J-7/JEDD via the CJCS JEL at http://www.dtic.mil/doctrine.

b. When a Joint Staff directorate submits a proposal to the Chairman of the Joint Chiefs of Staff that would change source document information reflected in this publication, that directorate will include a proposed change to this publication as an enclosure to its proposal. The Military Services and other organizations are requested to notify the Joint Staff/J-7 when changes to source documents reflected in this publication are initiated.

c. Record of Changes:

CHANGE NUMBER	COPY NUMBER	DATE OF CHANGE	DATE ENTERED	POSTED BY	REMARKS

4. Distribution Publications

Local reproduction is authorized and access to unclassified publications is unrestricted. However, access to and reproduction authorization for classified joint publications must be IAW DOD Regulation 5200.1-R, Information Security Program.

5. Distribution of Electronic Publications

a. Joint Staff J-7 will not print copies of JPs for distribution. Electronic versions are available on JDEIS at https://jdeis.js.mil (NIPRNET), and https://jdeis.js.smil.mil (SIPRNET) and on the JEL at http://www.dtic.mil/doctrine (NIPRNET).

b. Only approved joint publications and joint test publications are releasable outside the combatant commands, Services, and Joint Staff. Release of any classified joint publication to foreign governments or foreign nationals must be requested through the local embassy (Defense Attaché Office) to DIA Foreign Liaison Office, PO-FL, Room 1E811, 7400 Pentagon, Washington, DC 20301-7400.

c. CD-ROM. Upon request of a JDDC member, the Joint Staff J-7 will produce and deliver one CD-ROM with current joint publications.

GLOSSARY
PART I – ABBREVIATIONS AND ACRONYMS

ACC	Army Contracting Command
ACO	administrative contracting officer
ACSA	acquisition and cross-servicing agreement
AETC	Air Education and Training Command
AFB	Air Force base
AFCAP	Air Force Contract Augmentation Program
AFCESA	Air Force Civil Engineering Support Agency
AFMC	Air Force Materiel Command
AFRL	Air Force Research Laboratory
AFSB	Army field support brigade
ALT	acquisition, logistics, and technology
AOR	area of responsibility
ARFOR	Army forces
ASA(ALT)	Assistant Secretary of the Army for Acquisition, Logistics, and Technology
ASC	Army Sustainment Command
ASN(RD&A)	Assistant Secretary of the Navy for Research, Development and Acquisition
BOS	base operating support
C2	command and control
CAAF	contractors authorized to accompany the force
CAC	common access card
CAGO	contractor acquired government owned
CAP	civil augmentation program
CCAS	contingency contract administration services
CCDR	combatant commander
CCO	contingency contracting officer
CI	counterintelligence
CJCS	Chairman of the Joint Chiefs of Staff
CJCSM	Chairman of the Joint Chiefs of Staff manual
CLPSB	combatant commander logistic procurement support board
CMP	contractor management plan
COM	chief of mission
COR	contracting officer representative
CSB	contracting support brigade
CSIP	contract support integration plan
CUL	common-user logistics
DAR	Defense Acquisition Regulation
DCAA	Defense Contract Audit Agency
DCMA	Defense Contract Management Agency
DFARS	Department of Defense Federal Acquisition Regulation Supplement
DLA	Defense Logistics Agency

DOD	Department of Defense
DODD	Department of Defense directive
DODI	Department of Defense instruction
DOS	Department of State
DPAP	Defense Procurement and Acquisition Policy
DPMO	Defense Prisoner of War/Missing Personnel Office
DS	direct support
DSCA	defense support of civil authorities
EEDAC	emergency essential Department of the Army civilian
EPA	evasion plan of action
EPC	Emergency Procurement Committee
EPW	enemy prisoner of war
FAR	Federal Acquisition Regulation
FAST	field assessment surveillance team
FEMA	Federal Emergency Management Agency
FISC	fleet and industrial supply center
FM	field manual (Army)
FOIA	Freedom of Information Act
FOO	field ordering officer
FP	force protection
FRAGORD	fragmentary order
FSR	field service representative
GCC	geographic combatant commander
GCCC	Global Contingency Construction Contract
GCSC	Global Contingency Service Contract
GFE	government-furnished equipment
GPC	government purchase card
HCA	head of contracting activity
HN	host nation
HNS	host-nation support
HQ	headquarters
HQDA	Headquarters, Department of the Army
IA	individual augmentee
IAW	in accordance with
ICW	in coordination with
ID	identification
ID/IQ	indefinite delivery/indefinite quantity
IGE	independent government estimate
IGO	intergovernmental organization
J-1	manpower and personnel directorate of a joint staff

J-2	intelligence directorate of a joint staff
J-3	operations directorate of a joint staff
J-4	logistics directorate of a joint staff
J-5	plans directorate of a joint staff
J-6	communications system directorate of a joint staff
J-7	Joint Staff Operational Plans and Joint Force Development Directorate
JARB	joint acquisition review board
JCSB	joint contracting support board
JFC	joint force commander
JMD	joint manning document
JOA	joint operations area
JOPES	Joint Operation Planning and Execution System
JP	joint publication
JPME	joint professional military education
JRC	joint reception center
LCMC	life cycle management command
LOA	letter of authorization
LOGCAP	logistics civil augmentation program
LSU	logistics civil augmentation program support unit
MAGTF	Marine air-ground task force
MARCORSYSCOM	Marine Corps Systems Command
MILCON	military construction
MLSA	mutual logistics support agreement
MPS	Military Postal Service
MWR	morale, welfare, and recreation
NAE	Navy acquisition executive
NAVFAC	Naval Facilities Engineering Command
NAVSUPSYSCOM	Naval Supply System Command
NCF	naval construction force
NCO	noncommissioned officer
NG	National Guard
NGB	National Guard Bureau
NGO	nongovernmental organization
NURP	non-unit-related personnel
OGA	other government agency
OIF	Operation IRAQI FREEDOM
OPCON	operational control
OPLAN	operation plan
OPORD	operation order
OSD	Office of the Secretary of Defense

PCO	procuring contracting officer
PEO	program executive officer
PGI	procedures, guidance, and information
PM	program management
PN	partner nation
POW	prisoner of war
PR	personnel recovery
PWS	performance work statement
RCC	regional contracting center
RCO	regional contracting office
ROM	rough order of magnitude
RSOI	reception, staging, onward movement, and integration
RUF	rules for the use of force
SCO	senior contracting official
SDDC	Surface Deployment and Distribution Command
SecDef	Secretary of Defense
SF	standard form
SJA	staff judge advocate
SOF	special operations forces
SOFA	status-of-forces agreement
SOW	statement of work
SSTR	stability, security, transition, and reconstruction
SYSCOM	systems command
TCN	third country national
TPFDD	time-phased force and deployment data
UCMJ	Uniform Code of Military Justice
USAMC	United States Army Materiel Command
USC	United States Code
USD(AT&L)	Under Secretary of Defense for Acquisition, Technology, and Logistics
USD(P&R)	Under Secretary of Defense for Personnel and Readiness
USG	United States Government
USJFCOM	United States Joint Forces Command
USNORTHCOM	United States Northern Command
USPACOM	United States Pacific Command
USPFO(P&C)	United States Property and Fiscal Office (Purchasing and Contracting)
USSOCOM	United States Special Operations Command
USSOUTHCOM	United States Southern Command
USTRANSCOM	United States Transportation Command
UTC	unit type code

PART II – TERMS AND DEFINITIONS

Unless otherwise annotated, this publication is the proponent for all terms and definitions found in the glossary. Upon approval, JP 1-02, *Department of Defense Dictionary of Military and Associated Terms*, will reflect this publication as the source document for these terms and definitions.

administrative contracting officer. Contracting officer whose primary duties involve contract administration. Also called ACO. See also contracting officer; procuring contracting officer. (Approved for inclusion in JP 1-02.)

administrative lead time. None. (Approved for removal from JP 1-02.)

civil augmentation program. Standing, long-term external support contacts designed to augment Service logistic capabilities with contracted support in both preplanned and short notice contingencies. Examples include US Army Logistics Civil Augmentation Program, Air Force Contract Augmentation Program, and US Navy Global Contingency Capabilities Contracts. Also called CAP. See also contingency contract; external support contract. (This term and its definition modify the existing term and its definition and are approved inclusion in JP 1-02.)

classified contract. None. (Approved for removal from JP 1-02.)

combatant commander logistic procurement support board. A combatant commander-level joint board established to ensure that contracting support and other sources of support are properly synchronized across the entire area of responsibility. Also called CLPSB. See also joint acquisition review board; joint contracting support board. (Approved for inclusion in JP 1-02.)

contingency contract. A legally binding agreement for supplies, services, and construction let by government contracting officers in the operational area as well as other contracts that have a prescribed area of performance within a designated operational area. See also external support contract; systems support contract; theater support contract. (Approved for inclusion in JP 1-02.)

contingency contracting. The process of obtaining goods, services, and construction via contracting means in support of contingency operations. See also contingency contract. (This term and its definition modify the existing term and its definition and are approved inclusion in JP 1-02.)

contingency contractor personnel. None. (Approved for removal from JP 1-02.)

contract administration. A subset of contracting that includes efforts to ensure that supplies, services, and construction are delivered in accordance with the terms and conditions of the contract. (Approved for inclusion in JP 1-02.)

contracting officer. The Service member or Department of Defense civilian with the legal authority to enter into, administer, modify, and/or terminate contracts. (This term and its definition modify the existing term and its definition and are approved inclusion in JP 1-02.)

contracting officer representative. A Service member or Department of Defense civilian appointed in writing and trained by a contracting officer, responsible for monitoring contract performance and performing other duties specified by their appointment letter. Also COR. (Approved for inclusion in JP 1-02.)

contract maintenance. None. (Approved for removal from JP 1-02.)

contractor management. The oversight and integration of contractor personnel and associated equipment providing support to the joint force in a designated operational area. (Approved for inclusion in JP 1-02.)

contractors authorized to accompany the force. Contingency contractor employees and all tiers of subcontractor employees who are specifically authorized through their contract to accompany the force and have protected status in accordance with international conventions. Also called CAAF. (Approved for inclusion in JP 1-02.)

contractors deploying with the force. None. (Approved for removal from JP 1-02.)

contractors not authorized to accompany the force. Contingency contractor employees and all tiers of subcontractor employees who are not authorized through their contract to accompany the force and do not have protected status in accordance with international conventions. Also called non-CAAF. (Approved for inclusion in JP 1-02.)

contract support integration. The coordination and synchronization of contracted support executed in a designated operational area in support of the joint force. (Approved for inclusion in JP 1-02.)

contract termination. Defense procurement: the cessation or cancellation, in whole or in part, of work under a prime contract or a subcontract thereunder for the convenience of, or at the option of, the government, or due to failure of the contractor to perform in accordance with the terms of the contract (default). (JP 4-10)

cost-plus award fee contract. A type of contract that provides for a payment consisting of a base amount fixed at inception of the contract along with an award amount that is based upon a judgmental evaluation by the United States Government. (This term and its definition modify the existing term "cost-plus a fixed-fee contract" and its definition and are approved for inclusion in JP 1-02.)

cost sharing contract. None. (Approved for removal from JP 1-02.)

cost-type contract. A contract that provides for payment to the contractor of allowable cost, to the extent prescribed in the contract, incurred in performance of the contract. (This term and its definition modify the existing term "cost contract" and its definition and are approved inclusion in JP 1-02.)

delivery forecasts. None. (Approved for removal from JP 1-02.)

delivery requirements. None. (Approved for removal from JP 1-02.)

direct vendor delivery. A materiel acquisition and distribution method that requires vendor delivery directly to the customer. Also called DVD. (JP 4-09)

external support contract. Contract awarded by contracting organizations whose contracting authority does not derive directly from the theater support contracting head(s) of contracting activity or from systems support contracting authorities. See also systems support contract; theater support contract. (Approved for inclusion in JP 1-02.)

external support contractors. None. (Approved for removal from JP 1-02.)

field ordering officer. A Service member or Department of Defense civilian, who is appointed in writing and trained by a contracting officer and authorized to execute micropurchases in support of forces and/or designated civil-military operations. Also called FOO. (Approved for inclusion in JP 1-02.)

fixed price incentive contract. None. (Approved for removal from JP 1-02.)

fixed price type contract. A type of contract that generally provides for a firm price or, under appropriate circumstances, may provide for an adjustable price for the supplies or services being procured. Fixed price contracts are of several types so designed as to facilitate proper pricing under varying circumstances. (JP 4-10)

head of contracting activity. The official who has overall responsibility for managing the contracting activity. Also called HCA. (Approved for inclusion in JP 1-02.)

incentive type contract. None. (Approved for removal from JP 1-02.)

indefinite delivery type contract. None. (Approved for removal from JP 1-02.)

independent government estimate. The government's estimate of the resources and projected cost of the resources a contractor will incur in the performance of the contract. Also known as IGE. (Approved for inclusion in JP 1-02.)

industrial property. None. (Approved for removal from JP 1-02.)

initiation of procurement action. None. (Approved for removal from JP 1-02.)

interim financing. None. (Approved for removal from JP 1-02.)

isolated personnel. US military, Department of Defense civilians and contractor personnel (and others designated by the President or Secretary of Defense) who are separated from their unit (as an individual or a group) while participating in a US sponsored military activity or mission and are, or may be, in a situation where they must survive, evade, resist, or escape. (JP 3-50)

joint acquisition review board. A joint task force or subunified commander established board used to review and make recommendations for controlling critical common-user logistic supplies and services within the joint operational area and to recommend the proper sources of support for approved support requirements. Also called JARB. See also combatant commander logistic procurement support board; joint contracting support board. (Approved for inclusion in JP 1-02.)

joint contracting support board. A joint task force or subunified commander established board to coordinate all contracting support and to determine specific contracting mechanisms to obtain commercially procured common logistic supplies and services within the joint operational area. Also called JCSB. See also combatant commander logistic procurement support board; joint acquisition review board. (Approved for inclusion in JP 1-02.)

letter of authorization. A document issued by the procuring contracting officer or designee that authorizes contractor personnel authorized to accompany the force to travel to, from, and within the operational area; and, outlines government furnished support authorizations within the operational area. Also called LOA. (Approved for inclusion in JP 1-02.)

operational contract support. The process of planning for and obtaining supplies, services, and construction from commercial sources in support of joint operations along with the associated contractor management functions. (Approved for inclusion in JP 1-02.)

pecuniary liability. None. (Approved for removal from JP 1-02.)

performance work statement. A statement of work for performance based acquisitions that describe the results in clear, specific, and objective terms with measurable outcomes. Also called PWS. (Approved for inclusion in JP 1-02.)

prime contract. A contract or contractual action entered into by the United States Government for the purpose of obtaining supplies, materials, equipment, or services of any kind. (Approved for inclusion in JP 1-02.)

prime vendor. A contracting process that provides commercial products to regionally grouped military and federal customers from commercial distributors using electronic commerce. Customers typically receive materiel delivery through the vendor's commercial distribution system. Also called PV. See also direct vendor delivery. (JP 4-09)

privity of contract. The legal relationship that exists between two contracting parties, for example, between the government and the prime contractor. (Approved for inclusion in JP 1-02.)

procurement lead time. The interval in time between the initiation of procurement action and receipt into the supply system of the production model (excludes prototypes) purchased as the result of such actions. It is composed of two elements, production lead time and administrative lead time. (This term and its definition modify the existing term and its definition and are approved inclusion in JP 1-02.)

procuring contracting officer. A contracting officer who initiates and signs the contract. Also called PCO. See also administrative contracting officer; contracting officer. (Approved for inclusion in JP 1-02.)

production lead time. The time interval between the placement of a contract and receipt into the supply system of materiel purchased. Two entries are provided: a. **initial** — The time interval if the item is not under production as of the date of contract placement; and b. **reorder** — The time interval if the item is under production as of the date of contract placement. See also procurement lead time. (JP 4-10)

progress payment. None. (Approved for removal from JP 1-02.)

ratification. 1. The declaration by which a nation formally accepts, with our without reservation, the content of a standardization agreement. 2. The process of approving an unauthorized commitment by an official who has the authority to do so. See also unauthorized commitment. (This term and its definition modify the existing term and its definition and are approved inclusion in JP 1-02.)

receipt into the supply system. That point in time when the first item or first quantity of the item of the contract has been received at or is en route to point of first delivery after inspection and acceptance. See also procurement lead time. (JP 4-10)

requiring activity. A military or other designated supported organization that identifies and receives contracted support during military operations. See also supported unit. (Approved for inclusion in JP 1-02.)

senior contracting official. The lead Service or joint command designated contracting official who has direct managerial responsibility over theater support contracting. Also called SCO. (Approved for inclusion in JP 1-02.)

supported unit. As related to contracted support, a supported unit is the organization that is the recipient, but not necessarily the requester of, contractor-provided support. See also requiring activity. (Approved for inclusion in JP 1-02.)

systems support contract. A prearranged contract awarded by a Service acquisition program management office that provides technical support, maintenance and, in some cases, repair parts for selected military weapon and support systems. See also external support contract; theater support contract. (Approved for inclusion in JP 1-02.)

systems support contractors. None. (Approved for removal from JP 1-02.)

task order. Order for services placed against an established contract. See also civil augmentation program; cost-plus award fee contract. (Approved for inclusion in JP 1-02.)

theater support contract. A type of contingency contract that is awarded by contracting officers in the operational area serving under the direct contracting authority of the Service component, special operations force command, or designated joint head of contracting activity for the designated contingency operation. See also external support contract; systems support contract. (Approved for inclusion in JP 1-02.)

theater support contractors. None. (Approved for removal from JP 1-02.)

unauthorized commitment. An agreement that is not binding solely because the United States Government representative who made it lacked the authority to enter into that agreement on behalf of the Unites States Government. See also ratification. (Approved for inclusion in JP 1-02.)

JOINT DOCTRINE PUBLICATIONS HIERARCHY

JP 1
JOINT DOCTRINE

JP 1-0
PERSONNEL

JP 2-0
INTELLIGENCE

JP 3-0
OPERATIONS

JP 4-0
LOGISTICS

JP 5-0
PLANS

JP 6-0
COMMUNICATION SYSTEMS

All joint publications are organized into a comprehensive hierarchy as shown in the chart above. **Joint Publication (JP) 4-10** is in the **Logistics** series of joint doctrine publications. The diagram below illustrates an overview of the development process:

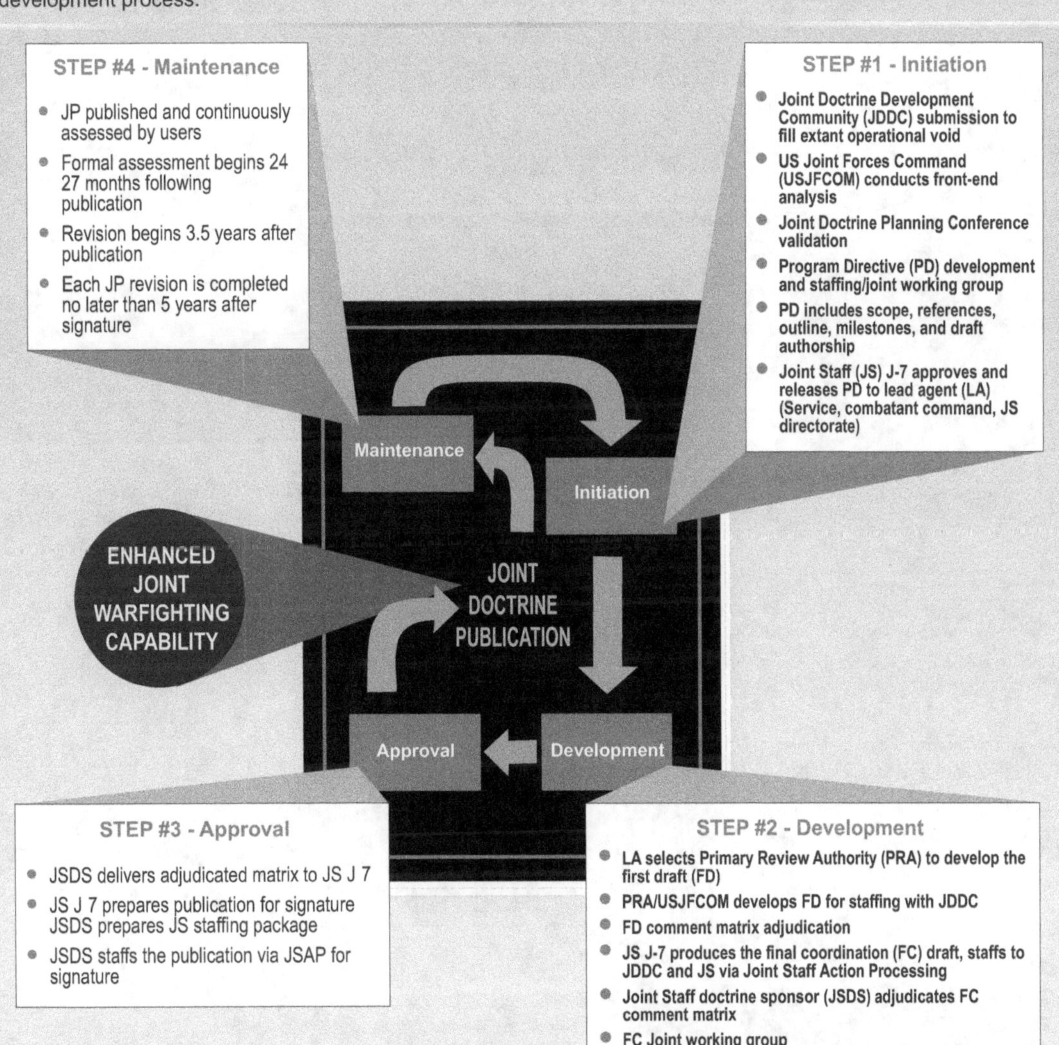

www.ingramcontent.com/pod-product-compliance
Lightning Source LLC
Chambersburg PA
CBHW081325310526
45789CB00018B/2366

* 9 7 8 1 5 0 0 6 6 2 2 3 3 *